More praise for *Baseball's All*

"Goats, chokers, bums — whatever you c
read and a great idea. Wish it was mine."
Rod Beaton, L

"Peter Weiss has produced a compelling collection. ...cball's 'goats' —
one that will both surprise you with some of the entries and put new twists on
some of the most traditional ones."
Harland Beery, *Bremerton (WA) Sun*

"Baseball's all-time goats may not be happy that Peter Weiss has kept their
blunders alive for eternity, but baseball fans should be thrilled. Unforgettable
moments and forgettable characters which fans have discussed for years are
now a collection for the ages."
Rich Chere, *The Star-Ledger*

"A valuable resource book which provides a rare and much-needed perspective."
David Cunningham, *Press-Telegram*

"Though the players featured may wish to be forgotten for their deeds, Peter
Weiss has rekindled memories with his descriptions of baseball's most famous
blunderers, ranging from the sport's earliest days to the most recent World Series."
Rob Dewolf, Sportswriter, *Canton Repository*

"Since it's not socially acceptable to laugh aloud at others' misfortunes, find a
nice, secluded place in which to read it."
Jeff Horrigan, *The National*

"You don't have to be a die-hard baseball fan to enjoy Peter Weiss'
recounting of some of the great moments in baseball's storied past. I found
Baseball's All-Time Goats hard to put down and was anxious to find out if
these so-called goats were really deserving of their tag."
Alan Hoskins
Sports Columnist, *Kansas City Kansan*

"This book produces a flood of memories and at times proves enlightening,
particularly the entry on Cap Anson."
Joe Illuzzi, *New York Post*

"Goats are more interesting than heroes. They're funnier, and they're more like us. All the goats are here — horns, little beards, and all."

Steve Jacobson, Columnist, *New York Newsday*

"They're all here, from Branca to Buckner, from Frazee to Finley — all the characters who have made 'goat-hood' a special tradition. A witty, entertaining, informative collection that shows the excruciating agony and heroic aspect of being on the wrong side for all-time."

Moss Klein, *Newark Star-Ledger*
Co-Author, *Damned Yankees*

"Nobody's perfect. But in baseball, nobody forgets, either."

Mark Langill, *Pasadena Star-News*

"From Anson to Wilson, from the daffy Dodgers to the disappointing Blue Jays, Peter Weiss has authored the ultimate baseball goat book."

Rich Marazzi
Author, *The Rules and Lore of Baseball*

"To err is human, and Peter Weiss proves it as he brings the goats and ghosts to life."

Ross Newhan
National Baseball Writer, *Los Angeles Times*

"There are so many goats in this book, you grow horns just reading it. I can't imagine going off to cover the postseason without it."

Jayson Stark
Baseball Columnist, *Philadelphia Inquirer*

"No group gets off — not owners, not umpires, not managers or, certainly, players such as Buckner and Owen, as baseball's greatest goats are skewered. Author Peter Weiss gives us a novel look at our national pastime that's great fun for all but the guilty."

Bill Tanton, Columnist, *Baltimore Evening Sun*

"A book to be read more than once. Yes, it is possible to write something new and fascinating about baseball."

Juan Vene, *El Diario*, New York

"One look at the lineup Peter Weiss has assembled here — from Babe Ruth to Jerry Dybzinski — tells you this is a unique baseball book. These tales of infamy, whether familiar or forgotten, are all worth revisiting."

Tom Verducci, Baseball Columnist, *Newsday*

Baseball's ALL-TIME Goats

As Chosen by
America's Top Sportswriters

PETER WEISS
Foreword by Dan Shaughnessy

BOB ADAMS, INC.
PUBLISHERS
Holbrook, Massachusetts

Published by Bob Adams, Inc.
260 Center Street, Holbrook, MA 02343

ISBN: 1-55850-104-5

Printed in the United States of America

A   B   C   D   E   F   G   H   I   J

COVER ILLUSTRATION: Paul Blumstein
GOAT ILLUSTRATIONS: Mike Lundin

Dedication

For Mom and Dad.
And for Melissa.

Table of Contents

Acknowledgments

First of all, this book wouldn't have been possible without the help of the hundreds of sportswriters who elected the all-time goats. Specifically, Bill Tanton of the *Baltimore Evening Sun* was very encouraging and helpful, as were John Kuenster of *Baseball Digest* and Ron Rapoport of the *Los Angeles Daily News*. Bruce Jenkins of the *San Francisco Chronicle* was nice enough to set up a "goat hotline" on his voice mail system and the *Bremerton Sun's* Harland Beery ran a similar "goat survey" in his column. Also, Kenny Hand of the *Houston Post* and Mel Durslag of Los Angeles each took the time to provide a funny quote.

Dan Shaughnessy of the *Boston Globe* deserves a hearty thanks for encouraging the project back when it was just an idea, for putting me in touch with all the sportswriters, and for contributing the foreword.

Much thanks go to publisher Bob Adams, who believed in the book's potential from Day One.

Michelle Bevilacqua, Bill Murphy, and Carter Smith each contributed to the book in one way or another and I thank them.

Thanks for their respective graphic expertise go out to: Chris Ciaschini, who did most of the layout work; and Mike Lundin, who created the illustrations.

Extra special thanks go to Brandon Toropov, who served as the book's "combat editor" and was great to work with. It is only fair to mention that on August 13, 1991, Brandon and I were involved in one of only a handful of triple plays in the history of company softball games. We were not on defense at the time.

I'd also like to thank: my brothers, Chris and Marc Weiss, for being overall good guys; my grandfather, Fred Coyle, who has spun some wild tales about the New York Yankees of the 1930's; Cathy, Peter, and Chris Winter, for completely redefining the concept of in-laws; Thomas Donahue and Thalia Selz for helping me learn how to write; Chris Harges, who knows a lot more about writing than he does about baseball; and Bill and Jody Buckner, for sitting down and talking about a subject that has grown quite stale in their household.

Finally, I must thank all of the ballplayers who appear in this book. Their only "mistake" was revealing that they are just as human as the rest of us.

Peter Weiss
Brookline, Massachusetts
December, 1991

Foreword

This book is overdue. There's a glut of baseball literature on the bookshelves, but until now, no author has told the stories of the men who've taken the blame for some of hardball's most celebrated moments.

It's easy to go through life being Bobby Thomson. He hit the "shot heard round the world" to end the 1951 season and deliver the pennant to the New York Giants. Thomson has been a hero since that day. Forty baseball seasons have come and gone, but time has not dimmed the memory of his deed. In some ways, Thomson's achievement grows larger every year.

But what's it like to be the man who threw the pitch? What's it like to go through life being Ralph Branca? What's it like to have people whisper about you when you go to the hardware store? What's it like to make business calls and have the person on the other end of the line ask, "Is this the Ralph Branca who threw the pitch?" When is enough enough? When does a man become a private citizen again, instead of a symbol of some failure from seasons past?

Peter Weiss' book, *Baseball's All-Time Goats*, explores this territory as never before. With help from America's baseball writers, Weiss has tackled the tough task of identifying baseball's most renowned goats. The list is expansive and thorough, and there are a few surprise entries.

It's fascinating to learn what happens to these athletes-of-infamy after they leave the field of play. We get a sense of how unfair it is to have a lengthy career remembered only for one unfortunate play, a bad day, or an ill-timed slump.

Baseball goats are largely symbolic. Did Red Sox first baseman Bill Buckner single-handedly lose the 1986 World Series? Of course not. Buckner made an error which resulted in the winning run crossing the plate in the sixth game of the Series, but that play alone did not lose the Series for Boston. The game was already tied when Mookie Wilson's grounder skipped between Buckner's legs. And even if Buckner had fielded the ball cleanly, there is no guarantee that the Red Sox would have won.

Two days after the error, the Sox blew a 3–0 lead in the seventh game of the Series. Despite all these messy facts, Buckner's error has gone down as the play that lost the World Series. It is a symbolic rather than a literal fact.

Years later, it's too hard to remember all the gory details of a seven-game series, but a grounder between the wickets is a tidy image of defeat. Buckner is Charlie Brown saying "Rats," after trying to kick the football and having Lucy pull the ball away. Buckner is the skier who tumbles off the jump platform at the beginning of "Wide World of Sports." Buckner is the agony of defeat. Nonstop television replay, selective memory, and slick packaging have conspired to make this hard-hitting first baseman the top goat in baseball history.

There are players who've been able to shed the goat horns before they ever took hold. We had an example of this in the historic third game of the 1991 World Series. It was after midnight in Atlanta and the Braves and Twins were tied, 4–4. Forty-two players were used in this game; with one on and one out in the 12th inning, Twins second baseman Chuck Knoblauch hit a grounder to Braves second baseman Mark Lemke. In his haste to turn a double play, Lemke booted the ball and the Twins had runners on first and third with one out. If Kent Hrbek had delivered, Lemke might have been the Bill Buckner of the South. Instead, Hrbek took a called third strike and Jim Clancy got Rick Aguilera for the third out. In the bottom of the inning, Lemke delivered a two-out single to score David Justice with the winning run.

In one short inning, Lemke went from goat to hero. He continued the heroism, scoring the winning run in Game 4, and hitting a pair of triples in Game 5. Braves fans hung banners reading, "Lemke for President."

Things went the other way for Lemke's teammate, Lonnie Smith. Smith was a member of three championship teams in the 1980's and he homered in three consecutive games in the 1991 Series. However, Smith's Game 7 baserunning blunder was the turning point in the unforgettable '91 Series. Smith was on first with no outs in the eighth inning of a scoreless game when Terry Pendleton ripped a double to left center. Smith started running with his head down, lost sight of the ball, and stopped after he got to second. He wound up at third, but should have scored. Jack Morris got out of the jam, the Twins won in ten innings, and Smith was awarded the goat horns.

Lonnie Smith joins the anti-heroes of this book. He will learn that bad news stays with us. There are thousands of successful airplane takeoffs and landings each year, but the crashes make news. Only the crashes are remembered.

The Dodgers' Willie Davis was a fine major league outfielder, but he's an eternal goat because he made three errors in one inning of one World Series game. As a big league manager, Gene Mauch won 1,902 games, but he's a goat because he never got to a World Series and his '64 Phillies blew a six and a half game lead with twelve to play. Johnny Pesky was a terrific shortstop and a .300 hitter, but for more than 45 years he's been a goat because he might have hesitated slightly with a relay throw in the 1946 World Series. None of this is very fair, but it's reality.

Red Sox pitcher Mike Torrez, who yielded the playoff-losing homer to Bucky Dent in 1978, never had much trouble accepting his place in the Boston pantheon of goats. However, when Buckner made his error in '86, Torrez was found in the bowels of Shea Stadium screaming, "I'm off the hook." Two years later, when Dent built a miniature Fenway Park for his Florida baseball school, Torrez graciously agreed to fly down and throw gopher pitches to Dent to celebrate the opening of the new park.

New York Giants first baseman Fred Merkle is probably the only goat who was strapped with a permanent nickname as a result of his gaffe. Merkle forgot to touch second base during a crucial play in the 1908 pennant race. He was accused of losing the flag for the Giants and to his dying day was known as "Bonehead" Merkle. How'd you like to be his grandson and have to tell people, "That's right, my granddad was old Bonehead himself." Was he really? We deserve an answer.

Peter Weiss' book offers a new perspective on all the "boneheads." We get to dissect the men and the moments. It's a new point of view and it's only fair. After all, goats are people, too.

Dan Shaughnessy
Newton, Massachusetts
November, 1991

How the Goats Were Selected

Starting in August 1991, we sent over 600 surveys out to America's leading sports journalists. The journalists were asked to list, in no particular order, who they felt to be the top ten baseball goats of all time. No guidelines for what constituted a goat were set; it was up to the journalist to determine what makes a goat.

The surveys poured in and our mailbox overflowed. Everyone seemed to have a favorite "home team" goat who needed proper recognition. Some journalists called and requested additional copies of the survey to distribute to colleagues.

We carefully tallied the results, assigning a point each time a person or team was mentioned in a survey. When all of the points were added up, we were able to "rank" the goats by computing from the total number of journalists surveyed the percentage that mentioned the person or team.

What follows are forty-one chapters devoted to the top goats of all time according to our survey. In an attempt to maintain objectivity, these chapters are presented alphabetically. To find out the ranking of these all-time goats, see the chapter entitled "The Survey Results" starting on page 185.

THE GOATS

Adrian Constantine "Cap" Anson
Chicago White Stockings
1876–1897

CAREER HIGHLIGHTS

YEAR	TEAM	AVG	G	AB	R	H	2B	3B	HR	RBI
1881	Chicago	.399	84	343	67	137	21	7	1	82
1884	Chicago	.335	112	475	108	159	30	3	21	102
1886	Chicago	.371	125	504	117	187	35	11	10	147
1887	Chicago	.347	122	472	107	164	33	13	7	102
1888	Chicago	.344	134	515	101	177	20	12	12	84
1892	Chicago	.272	146	559	62	152	25	9	1	74
1894	Chicago	.388	83	340	82	132	28	4	5	99
	CAREER TOTALS	.329	2276	9101	1719	2995	528	124	97	1879

No one can deny that Cap Anson's accomplishments on the field were stellar. He hit .300 or better twenty-five times in a twenty-two-year career. He led the National League in runs batted in eight times. He amassed a then-unprecedented 2,995 career hits. What's more, there is no famous, big-stakes, title-on-the-line game situation in which he came up short and earned any lasting measure of infamy.

Why then, would he be ranked among the game's all-time goats? The answer is simple and sobering. Anson was an early and influential proponent of the idea that blacks had no business playing major league baseball.

Cap Anson was, to his credit, the greatest hitter of his day; yet he was, much to his discredit, an inveterate racist who used his position of primacy in the game to advance the principle that (quoting Anson now) "gentlemen do not play baseball with niggers." That attitude was not universally accepted in the 1880s, when Anson was playing. He shares much of the responsibility for the "color line" hardening into major-league tradition as the twentieth century dawned. And it is difficult not to conclude that Anson was proud of that.

The Chicago White Stockings had a black mascot named Clarence Duval. In his autobiography, Anson jovially refers to Duval as a "coon," a "no-account nigger," and a "little darkie." He relates that Duval was forced to bathe upon joining the team, and reports that he "fought tooth and nail" to avoid such a fate. Such racist stereotyping is fully in keeping with other incidents in Anson's career.

In late July of 1884, for instance, Anson's White Stockings were to face the Toledo franchise of the American Association. The Toledo catcher was a popular black player named Moses Walker; Anson caught sight of him in uniform and insisted to the Toledo management that either Walker be removed from the field or Chicago would not play. (The game was eventually played under protest.)

Another such incident is recorded during the 1888 season. Black pitcher George Stovey was scheduled to pitch for Newark against Chicago. Anson, the reigning star of the day and primary box-office attraction in big-league baseball, refused to play unless Newark removed Stovey from the game. This time Cap won; Stovey withdrew of his own accord and the game went on as scheduled.

Many fans are surprised to learn that professional baseball in the very early days of the game had a variety of approaches to the issue of black ballplayers; some leagues allowed them, and some didn't. Cap Anson was an unyielding advocate of strict racial segregation on the field, however, and he made his position quite clear to National League officials. By the early 1890's, his arguments had carried the day. It is an interesting question whether the ban on black players would have gained acceptance if the dominant player of the era had not been the tireless advocate of white-only play that he was.

Anson's racist standards held sway until 1947, when Jackie Robinson broke the color barrier with the Brooklyn Dodgers.

The Verdict

Some of the biggest mistakes in baseball take place off the field, and segregation ranks at the top of the list. Anson's unyielding racist attitudes were a dishonor to the game and a blemish on his own remarkable playing career.

Larry Barnett

Umpire
American League
1975 World Series
Boston Red Sox *vs.* Cincinnati Reds

On October 14, 1975, Larry Barnett may well have been a little nervous as he stepped behind home plate and yelled, "Play ball!" He had been umpiring in the American League for eight years, and this was his first time running the show from behind the plate in a World Series game. Before the night was over, Barnett's blown call involving Boston Red Sox catcher Carlton Fisk and Cincinnati Red pinch hitter Ed Armbrister would add just the right amount of obligatory controversy to perhaps the greatest World Series of all time.

The Red Sox and Reds had split the first two games at Boston's Fenway Park before making the trip to Cincinnati's Riverfront Stadium. By the end of the fifth inning of Game 3, the Reds had a 5–1 lead thanks to home runs by Johnny Bench, Cesar Geronimo, and Dave Concepcion.

But Boston battled back with a seventh-inning pinch-homer from Bernie Carbo (his first of two in the Series) and a dramatic two-run blast in the ninth by Dwight Evans to tie it up. The Reds couldn't push a run across in the bottom of the ninth; the game went to extra innings.

Geronimo led off the tenth with a single. The soon-to-be immortal Edison Rosanda Armbrister, who flirted with a .190 average during the regular season, came to the plate with explicit directions to do one thing: lay down a sacrifice bunt. With the infield drawn in, he proceeded as instructed and bounced the pitch off the plate. Boston catcher Carlton Fisk tried to grab the ball, but Armbrister didn't move toward first. The two collided and shoved each other for a moment before Fisk finally snagged the ball and hurled it wildly into center field. Geronimo zipped over to third and Armbrister wound up at second. Fisk was charged with an error.

The Red Sox couldn't believe that no interference had been called—Armbrister had waited for what seemed like years before heading to first base! Sox manager Darrell Johnson jawed with Barnett, but wasn't very feisty. Johnson reportedly never made any logical argument about the call, simply repeating vague dissatisfaction: "I don't like your operation here. This is a lousy operation, I tell ya . . . I just don't like it . . ." Barnett held strong, maintaining that Armbrister hadn't intentionally hampered Fisk's throw. Slow motion replays indicated otherwise to many observers.

The game continued. Roger Moret became the fifth Boston pitcher of the game and got the hellish inning's first out. But then Joe Morgan knocked one over centerfielder Fred Lynn's head to win the nerve-wracking contest and put the Reds up 2–1 in the Series. The Reds went on to win the see-saw series in seven games.

For many, the '75 World Series was about as close as you can get to perfection. It had drama, suspense, humor, thrills, spills—but it needed a goat to be a true classic. Barnett played the role beautifully. The Armbrister incident was the only real occurance of controversy in any of the seven games. But it hung like a cloud over the Series, and indeed over Barnett's career in the years to come.

The Verdict

The rulebook states, "It is interference by a batter or runner when, in the judgment of the umpire, a batter-runner willfully and deliberately interferes with a batted ball or a fielder in the act of fielding a batted ball . . ." Replays made it clear enough to most baseball people that Armbrister willfully blocked Fisk in the act of fielding a batted ball. Failing to call interference was a poor judgment call on Barnett's part, and to this day Fisk maintains he would have had a sure double play if Armbrister hadn't hesitated running to first. Barnett's position on this list is well-deserved.

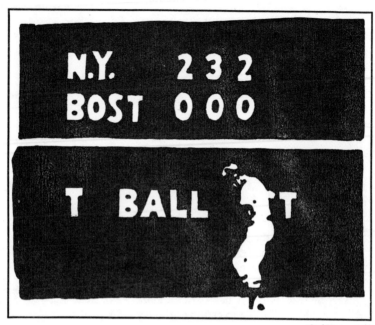

N.Y. 232
BOST 000

T BALL T

Carl Yastrzemski

Boston Red Sox
The 1978 Season

AMERICAN LEAGUE EAST STANDINGS, JULY 20, 1978

Team	W	L	Pct.	GB
Boston	62	28	.689	—
Milwaukee	53	37	.589	9
Baltimore	51	42	.548	12½
New York	49	42	.538	13½

FINAL AMERICAN LEAGUE EAST STANDINGS, 1978

Team	W	L	Pct.	GB
New York	100	63	.613	—
Boston	99	64	.607	1
Milwaukee	93	69	.574	6½
Baltimore	90	71	.559	9

In 1987, the Toronto Blue Jays figured out a way to lose their final seven games and the divisional title. The 1964 Philadelphia Phillies led by six and a half with twelve games left and blew it. The 1951 Brooklyn Dodgers blew a thirteen game lead on August 11. There is no doubt that these infamous collapses were heartbreaking for their fans.

But these were steady, seemingly inexorable descents. In 1978, the Boston Red Sox didn't just break their fans' hearts. They tortured them at length by collapsing, recovering, and then collapsing again.

The '78 Sox put up some big numbers. Newly acquired pitcher Dennis Eckersley had a career year (20–8, 2.99), and free agent acquisition Mike Torrez (16–13, 3.96) had a great first half though he floundered after the All-Star break. As far as hitting went, the big contributor was leftfielder/designated hitter Jim Rice, who would beat out Yankee ace Ron Guidry for the MVP title. Rice had the most total bases in the majors in thirty years with 406. He also led the AL in eight major batting categories including home runs (46), runs batted in (139), hits (213), and slugging percentage (.600). There were other offensive stars. Future Hall of Famer Carl Yastrzemski batted .277 with 17 homers. Gold Glove winner Dwight Evans began to show power at the plate by contributing 24 round trippers. Newly acquired second baseman Jerry Remy brought rare speed to the Sox and stole 30 bases while batting .278.

Things looked just about wrapped up by the end of the first half of the season. The Red Sox were the most dominant team in baseball, playing .850-plus ball at Fenway. On July 20, they led the Brewers by 9 games and the ragged Yankees by 13½ (see table).

But many observers questioned Boston manager Don Zimmer's tactics. For one, he was playing his regulars into the ground. In addition, Zimmer held strange grudges, avoiding using key players (notably pitcher Bill Lee). But the real problem was rest for hurt players. As the season progressed, injuries took their toll on Boston, though Zimmer seemed not to notice. Evans was beaned and suffered dizziness—but he only missed a few games. Shortstop Rick Burleson hurt his ankle and was allowed only minimal time off. Jerry Remy's wrist was shot. He played anyway. Fred Lynn and Carlton Fisk had various ailments but saw little rest. And Yastrzemski was plagued with problems in his back and wrist. He, too, remained in the lineup.

Third baseman Butch Hobson's bum elbow kicked in and he lost the ability to throw a ball into the first baseman's mitt. Again and again Hobson would charge a grounder, field it slickly, and finish the play by side-arming the ball into the upper seats of section 13 at Fenway Park. But he still played every day, demonstrating the "Aw, he'll get over it" attitude Zim was rapidly becoming famous for. By season's end, Hobson would shatter the record for errors by a third baseman.

The Sox started slumping in the second half, posting a disastrous road trip after the All-Star break.

Meanwhile in New York, fiery Yankee manager Billy Martin had been replaced by Bob Lemon. Infielders Bucky Dent and Willie Randolph, who were hurt earlier in the season, returned. Captain Thurman Munson felt good enough to return to catching after a stint in the less-rigorous right field position. With new blood and renewed vigor, the Yanks started winning ballgames—and gaining ground.

It helped that Don Zimmer's pitching staff was falling apart. Zimmer-nemesis Bill Lee was sent out to pasture in the bullpen after a tough outing, more out of spite than anything. Lee later told the *Boston Herald*, "His exact words to me were: 'We'll win without you.' Every manager has a doghouse, but Zimmer's doghouse had no door on it. You go in and you never get out."

Torrez struggled, losing late-inning games at home and on the road. Eckersley still had his stuff, but suddenly received little offensive support and began dropping tough games.

The Bronx Bombers were only four games behind on September 7, when they came to Fenway for a crucial four-game showdown. What happened at Fenway Park over those four days was one of the most lopsided four-game series in baseball history. New York swept Boston, and how, outscoring the Sox by a combined score of 42–9. Boston committed 12 errors, mostly of the Hobson variety. The Yanks moved into a first-place tie.

In the final month of the season, however, Boston got it together, keeping pace with New York all the way. With each team down to one game left to play, New York was alone in first by one game. As though divine right meant to salvage the Boston season, the lowly Cleveland Indians beat the Yankees 9–2 while the Red Sox shut out the Toronto Blue Jays 5–0. The season thus ended in a first-place tie, each team posting a record of 99–63. A one-game playoff would decide the division champion.

At Fenway Park, the heartbreak was completed. The Yankees pulled off a come-from behind win highlighted by the now-famous Bucky Dent pop-fly three-run homer (see chapter on Mike Torrez). Later, with two out and runners on in the bottom of the ninth, his team down by one, Yastrzemski came to the plate and popped up on the second pitch to end an agonizing rollercoaster season for the Red Sox. After the game, Fisk said of Yaz's high pop up, "I was trying to will the ball to stay up there and never come down." It didn't work. The Yankees went on to win the World Series.

The Verdict

Torrez got a lot of blame for this one—giving up the crucial home run to a non-power hitter—but there's no way you can pin 1978 on one guy. Credit the Yankees for an amazing comeback, but blame the entire Red Sox team, and especially Don Zimmer, for the collapse. The Red Sox were able to beat themselves in 1978, a feat they would repeat in 1986.

Ralph Branca

Pitcher, Brooklyn Dodgers
National League Playoff *vs.* New York Giants
October 3, 1951

YEAR	TEAM	W	L	G	GS	IP	H	HR	BB	SO	ERA
1944	Dodgers	0	2	21	1	45	46	2	32	16	7.00
1945	Dodgers	5	6	16	15	110	73	4	79	69	3.03
1946	Dodgers	3	1	24	10	67	62	4	41	42	3.90
1947	Dodgers	21	12	43	36	280	251	22	98	148	2.67
1948	Dodgers	14	9	36	28	216	189	24	80	122	3.50
1949	Dodgers	13	5	34	27	187	181	21	91	109	4.38
1950	Dodgers	7	9	43	15	142	152	24	55	100	4.69
1951	Dodgers	13	12	42	27	204	180	19	85	118	3.26
1952	Dodgers	4	2	16	7	61	52	8	21	26	3.84
1953	Dodgers	0	0	7	0	11	15	4	5	5	9.82
1953	Tigers	4	7	17	14	102	98	7	31	50	4.15
1954	Tigers	3	3	17	5	45	63	10	30	15	5.80
1954	Yankees	1	0	5	3	13	9	0	13	7	2.77
1956	Dodgers	0	0	1	0	2	1	0	2	2	0.00
	TOTALS	88	68	322	188	1485	1372	149	663	829	3.79

The Brooklyn Dodgers had just watched their 13½-game mid-August lead disappear at the hands of the surging New York Giants, who went a remarkable 37–7 down the stretch. At the end of the season the two teams were locked in a tie for first place. A three-game "mini-series" between the two clubs would be played to determine the pennant-winner.

At Ebbets Field, the Giants won the tight first game by a score of 3–1. Dodger right-hander Ralph Branca took the tough loss, giving up a two-run homer to slugging Giant third baseman Bobby Thomson. The second game was a Brooklyn blowout: The Dodgers stomped on everything the Giants had to offer and won 10–0. The third and deciding game would determine the outcome of the season.

Fans at the Polo Grounds were in a frenzy on October 3, 1951; the winner of this game would go on to challenge the Yankees in yet another subway World Series. The Dodgers held a comfortable 4–1 lead going into the bottom of the ninth.

A late rally got underway when Whitey Lockman doubled in a run for the Giants. That was the end for starter Don Newcombe. With two on, one out, and his team now ahead 4–2, young Dodger Ralph Branca—wearing uniform number 13—was summoned from the bullpen to put out the fire. The winning run was at the plate in the form of Bobby Thomson—the same Bobby Thomson who had homered off Branca in Game One.

Branca burned a fastball down the pipe for a called first strike. The plan was to deliver another fastball, this time up and in, in order to fool Thomson with a low and away curve for the next pitch.

Branca never got to try his tricky third pitch. Thomson connected with the high inside fastball for a screaming three-run homer to win the game and the league championship. Giants radio announcer Russ Hodges could only scream over and over, "The Giants win the pennant! The Giants win the pennant!"

Nearly every baseball fan has seen the grainy black and white footage of Thomson being swarmed by fans and teammates while attempting to round the bases after his pennant-winning home run. To call Thomson's homer dramatic is like calling *Gone With The Wind* a decent home movie.

After the game, the entire Brooklyn team was in shock. The whole of the 1951 season had been swept out from under them. Branca couldn't speak; he slumped on the clubhouse steps and looked at the ground. But since that fateful day, Branca dealt with his status admirably. He has often said that his pitch was where he wanted it to be, and that Thomson was simply on top of it.

Ironically, Branca and Thomson have become close friends over the years, sharing family outings and making frequent public appearances together.

The Verdict

To be sure, Branca did his job. He got the pitch
up and in—out of the strike zone—right where it
was supposed to be. Thomson simply cranked it
into the left field stands. It's probably just as fair
to remember Thomson as a dramatic hero as to
remember Branca as the pitcher who lost Brooklyn a pennant. But for our purposes, Branca's
second home run offering to the dangerous
Thomson in three games earns him a secure position
on the all-time goat list.

Lou Brock
Outfield, St. Louis Cardinals
1968 World Series *vs.* Detroit Tigers

CAREER HIGHLIGHTS

YEAR	TEAM	AVG	G	AB	R	H	2B	3B	HR	RBI	SB
1962	Cubs	.263	123	434	73	114	24	7	9	35	16
1963	Cubs	.258	148	547	79	141	19	11	9	37	24
1964	Cardinals	.348	103	419	81	146	21	9	12	44	33
1965	Cardinals	.288	155	631	107	182	35	8	16	69	63
1966	Cardinals	.285	156	643	94	183	24	12	15	46	74
1967	Cardinals	.299	159	689	113	206	32	12	21	76	52
1968	Cardinals	.279	159	660	92	184	46	14	6	51	62
1969	Cardinals	.298	157	655	97	195	33	10	12	47	53
1970	Cardinals	.304	155	664	114	202	29	5	13	57	51
1971	Cardinals	.313	157	640	126	200	37	7	7	61	64
1972	Cardinals	.311	153	621	81	193	26	8	3	42	63
1973	Cardinals	.297	160	650	110	193	29	8	7	63	70
1974	Cardinals	.306	153	635	105	194	25	7	3	48	118
1975	Cardinals	.309	136	528	78	163	27	6	3	47	56
1976	Cardinals	.301	133	498	73	150	24	5	4	67	56
1977	Cardinals	.272	141	489	69	133	22	6	2	46	35
1979	Cardinals	.304	120	405	56	123	15	4	5	38	21
CAREER TOTALS		.293	2616	10332	1610	3023	486	141	149	900	938

As in the case of one-time home run king Babe Ruth, (see separate chapter), people seem to have forgotten that one-time stolen base king, Lou Brock, had moments that earned him a spot as one of baseball's all-time goats. It seems on two separate occasions in the 1968 World Series, the Hall of Famer pushed his luck too far.

Brock's team, the St. Louis Cardinals, were the favorites to win the Series. This was the year of the pitcher, and the Cards had one, Bob Gibson, who had just set a modern record that year with a superhuman ERA of 1.12. Unlike most of the rest of the majors, St. Louis also had some solid offense in players like Brock, Orlando Cepeda, Curt Flood, and Tim McCarver.

The Cards were matched up against the Detroit Tigers, who had won 103 games that year, but didn't really have much in the offense department. In a year when the entire American League batted only .230 and batting champ Carl Yastrzemski hit only .301, the Tigers were relying on their pitching to give them a chance against the Cardinals.

The Series started on October 2. In Game 1, Bob Gibson carried St. Louis past 31-game winner Denny McLain and the Tigers by a 4–0 score. Brock hit a home run and Gibson struck out an amazing 17 batters—still a record in World Series play. But Game 2 was quite a different beast. Tiger pitcher Mickey Lolich pitched a masterful complete game, winning 8–1 and smashing a home run himself.

The Series moved to Detroit, where the Cards took Games 3 and 4 to come within a game of the world championship. Brock had contributed another homer in Game 4 as Gibson had smoked McLain, 10–1, for the second time in a week. The Tigers were face to face with a long winter.

In the fifth inning of Game 5, the Tigers were down 3–2. St. Louis looked to add some insurance when Lou Brock doubled with one out. Second baseman Julian Javier then singled to left center. Detroit left fielder Willie Horton rifled a strike to catcher Bill Freehan. Brock, then far and away the best base runner in either league, might have felt overconfident in trying to score from second base, for he elected *not* to slide into home. Quite a gamble; Brock weighed a paltry 170 pounds compared to Bill's 205-pound girth. Freehan successfully blocked the plate and Brock was the second out of the inning. The Tigers went ahead 5–3 in the seventh on Al Kaline's bases-loaded single and hung on the win the game. Critics argued that Brock's decision not to slide killed the rally, and was the turning point of the game.

With newfound vigor, McLain and the Tigers romped in Game 6. They cranked out ten runs in the third inning, finally winning, 13–1. The Series would go to a seventh and deciding game.

With no score in the bottom of the sixth inning of Game 7, Brock made his second big mistake of the Series. He singled to left and taunted Detroit pitcher Mickey Lolich by taking a huge lead. Brock had stolen second twice off Lolich in Game 2; perhaps overconfidence played a role again. Lolich, whose ability to hold runners on was suspect, heard second baseman Dick McAuliffe and first baseman Norm Cash shouting at him. Later, he said, "I didn't know whether they were telling me to step off or throw over, but I decided I'd better throw over to first." He did; Brock tried to steal anyway. Cash fired the ball to second with plenty of time, and Brock was a goner. Later in the inning, Curt Flood was picked off at first in a similar play. Lolich told reporters he had never picked off two runners in one game, let alone one inning. The Tiger turnaround was complete, and the adrenalin-pumped Lolich finished off the Cardinals, the game, and the World Series.

Disappointed St. Louis fans looked for a scapegoat and found Lou Brock, the best base runner in the game who would later set the record for lifetime stolen bases.

The Verdict

It's unfair to label Brock the goat of the 1968 World Series for one major reason: his running gaffes weren't the direct cause of any of his team's losses. Moreover, he led his team's regulars with a .464 Series average with two key home runs. The '68 Series shouldn't be remembered for having a goat who "lost the Series." If anything, it should be remembered for having a hero, Mickey Lolich, who led the Tigers to the championship.

Preacher Roe

Brooklyn Dodgers
1951 Season Finish

1951 NATIONAL LEAGUE FINAL STANDINGS/TEAM STATS
(bold/underline indicates league leader)

	W	L	PCT	GB	R	H	HR	AVG
New York Giants	**98**	**59**	**.624**	—	781	1396	179	.260
Brooklyn Dodgers	97	60	.618	1	**855**	**1511**	**184**	**.275**

It wasn't easy being a Dodger fan in the early '50's. Four times between 1947 and 1953 "dem bums" met the New York Yankees in the World Series—and four times they lost to the hated Yanks. Then there were all the agonizing photo-finishes to reach the Series in the first place. When would it all end?

In 1950, the Dodgers had teased their fans by mounting an amazing stretch run to catch the suddenly-floundering Philadelphia Phillies. They wound up going into the last game of the season in a virtual first-place tie with the Phils, who had had a woeful September. The last game was between the two first-place teams; the Dodgers lost it in the tenth inning.

But it was during the next season, 1951, that the Dodgers drove a stake through the hearts of their followers. At the beginning of the season, the Dodgers were playing awesome ball. Their lineup included such legendary names as Jackie Robinson, Duke Snider, and Gil Hodges. And their pitching staff was solid throughout, featuring Don Newcombe, Preacher Roe, and Carl Erskine. By mid-season, the Dodgers were so far ahead of the pack that things looked to be about wrapped up in the National League.

The Dodgers' crosstown rivals, the New York Giants, had gotten off to a very shaky start. With former Brooklyn manager Leo Durocher at the helm, the team lost its first eleven games and spent months playing catch-up. But things eventually evened out. Late in the season, the Giants found their groove and tore off sixteen straight wins starting on August 12.

At the start of their incredible streak, they were a whopping 13½ games behind Brooklyn, but steadily the Giants caught up. With one game left to play in the regular season, the odyssey was nearly complete; the two teams were tied for first place. Each team won its respective final game in dramatic fashion—the Dodgers in extra-innings against the Phillies.

The regular season ended, and both teams were still locked in a first-place tie. The Dodgers and Giants got set to play a best-of-three-game playoff series to decide who would face the American League champions, the Yankees.

The teams split the first two games. Going into the ninth inning of the deciding game, Brooklyn led 4–1, but collapsed under a New York rally capped by Bobby Thomson's "shot heard 'round the world" homer in the bottom of the ninth inning (see chapter on Ralph Branca).

The seemingly insurmountable 13½-game cushion had vanished in a twinkling. For the second time in two years, the Dodgers had lost the National League pennant in the final inning of the final game of the season.

The next day, Red Smith wrote in the *New York Herald Tribune*: "Now it is done . . . now the story ends. And there is no way to tell it. The art of fiction is dead. Reality has strangled invention. Only the utterly impossible, the inexpressibly fantastic, can ever be plausible again." It would be four years before the inexpressibly fantastic World Series of 1955, in which the Dodgers finally toppled the mighty Yankees.

The Verdict

No goats here. It was the Giants' incredible September drive that won the pennant in '51, not the Dodgers' collapse. Brooklyn played at a .500-plus clip towards the end.

Bill Buckner

First Base, Boston Red Sox
World Series *vs.* New York Mets
October 25, 1986

CAREER HIGHLIGHTS

YEAR	TEAM	AVG	G	AB	R	H	2B	3B	HR	RBI
1974	Dodgers	.314	145	580	83	182	30	3	7	58
1978	Cubs	.323	117	446	47	144	26	1	5	74
1980	Cubs	.324	145	578	69	187	41	3	10	68
1982	Cubs	.306	161	657	93	201	34	5	15	105
1985	Red Sox	.299	162	673	89	201	46	3	16	110
1986	Red Sox	.267	153	629	73	168	39	2	18	102
	CAREER TOTALS	.289	2517	9397	1077	2715	498	49	174	1208

Bill Buckner's career in the major leagues, which spanned four decades, was a rollercoaster ride through some of the most bizarre, triumphant, and fateful events in baseball history. As a minor leaguer in the late 1960s, he played for Tom Lasorda and roomed with Bobby Valentine. He scrambled up the left field wall in vain as Hank Aaron's record-breaking 715th home run sailed over his head in 1974. He constantly faced injury problems and nearly had to have his foot amputated in 1976, but came back stronger than ever. He hit over .300 seven times, won the batting title in 1980, and is ranked 40th on the all-time hits chart. But it isn't for any of these achievements that he is remembered.

It was Buckner's role in the 1986 World Series that most people recall. His team, the Boston Red Sox, had not won a world championship since 1918, but had clawed their way to a three-to-two game advantage in the Series against the heavily favored New York Mets.

So it was that in the bottom of the tenth inning of Game 6, the Red Sox, ahead 5–3, were within one inning of winning it all. The champagne was waiting in the locker room, the team's octogenarian owner had already been presented with a plaque, and Bruce Hurst, the Red Sox' star lefty, had been named the Series MVP. "Congratulations to the World Champion Red Sox" flashed on the Shea Stadium scoreboard.

Then the tide turned. Three singles yielded by Calvin Schiraldi sliced the Red Sox' two-run lead in half. Bob Stanley came in from the bullpen, brought the Sox within a single strike of the championship, but then threw a wild pitch to tie the score. Finally, Mookie Wilson's slow, dribbling grounder found its way through Bill Buckner's legs and under his glove, allowing the winning run to score. The Mets had come back to win the game—and eventually the Series. Buckner became a hated man in Boston.

The next season, Bill was released by the Red Sox, bounced around the American League, and was booed every time he returned to Fenway Park as an opponent. In just one year, he went from hustling veteran superstar to "the guy who blew the Series."

There seemed to be a happy ending in sight, however, as Buckner decided to make peace with Boston. In February 1990, Buckner—forty years old and without a team—petitioned the Red Sox to give him a spring training tryout. Claiming he was in his best shape in ten years and ready to help the Sox win the 1990 World Series, Buckner was given little chance to make the team. He never relented, however, and was eventually given a tryout in a local high school gym. Most fans were still bitter about 1986, but the Red Sox front office wondered whether it might not have something. Buckner was invited to spring training, where he outhit and outran players half his age and eventually made the team. He got a memorable and emotional welcome home on Opening Day 1990, receiving a standing ovation at Fenway Park.

There is no storybook ending, however. In early May of the 1990 campaign, the Red Sox gave Buckner his outright release. Even though he didn't get his chance to play in another World Series, Bill ended his career in a Red Sox uniform and seemed to have earned a measure of the fans' forgiveness.

The Verdict

In the nationwide survey conducted to generate our list of all-time goats, Buckner ran away with the top vote-getting "honors." But his case is one that deserves closer scrutiny. Just five years after Buckner's well-publicized blunder, even some of the top sportswriters in the country seem to have forgotten that the Sox had already allowed the Mets to tie the game when the error occured. Furthermore, it is usually forgotten that there were two other Red Sox errors earlier in the game, as well as a wild pitch. It stands to reason that even if Buckner had made the putout to send the game to the eleventh, the Mets' momentum might very well have carried the day for them anyway.

Jose Canseco
Outfield
Oakland Athletics
World Series *vs.* Los Angeles Dodgers
October 15–20, 1988

YEAR	TEAM	AVG	G	AB	R	H	2B	3B	HR	RBI
1985	A's	.302	29	96	16	29	3	0	5	13
1986	A's	.240	157	600	85	144	29	1	33	117
1987	A's	.257	159	630	81	162	35	3	31	113
1988	A's	.307	158	610	120	187	34	0	42	124
1989	A's	.269	65	227	40	61	9	1	17	57
1990	A's	.274	131	481	83	132	14	2	37	101
1991	A's	.266	154	572	115	152	32	1	44	122
	CAREER TOTALS	.270	853	3216	540	867	156	8	209	647

In 1988 as today, Jose Canseco was a big star who took his fame very seriously. A cocky personality who knew what he was worth, Jose charged outrageous fees for autograph-signing appearances and had been known to arrive late to spring training because of his demanding personal appearance schedule. At one point, he even set up a "1-900" hotline so that his fans could pay money to listen to him hold forth about a number of topics — usually focusing on himself.

Baseball fans and collectors certainly had mixed feelings about his behavior, but no one could deny his talent as a hitting powerhouse. His 42 home runs and 124 RBI's were tops in the majors in 1988. And his 40 stolen bases made him the first major leaguer to pull off a "40–40" season. The card-show circuit ate it up as his rookie baseball card from just two years earlier shot up in value from $10 to an astonishing $60.

Canseco's team, the Oakland Athletics dominated the majors that year, going 104–58 and leaving the second-place Twins a cool thirteen games back. When October rolled around, the A's steamrolled the Red Sox in the playoffs, sweeping the four-game series. Canseco joined in the romp, going 5 for 16 with three key home runs. Oakland was the odds-on favorite to destroy the Los Angeles Dodgers in the World Series.

Jose started the 1988 World Series off with a bang. In the second inning of Game 1, he continued his power tear by blasting a grand slam off Tim Belcher. Folks took this as a preview of a Dodger trouncing, but quite the opposite occurred. The Dodgers came back to win the first game 5–4 on Kirk Gibson's dramatic ninth inning homer (see chapter on Dennis Eckersley).

After his monster grand slam, Canseco had 20 more plate appearances in the Series. He would not get another hit. The man who reduced opposing pitchers to dust during the regular season couldn't muster another base hit in the four biggest games of his career up to that point. His World Series average ended up a miniscule .053. The Dodgers took the championship from Oakland four games to one, and sent Canseco out to graze for the winter.

The Verdict

Jose Canseco is definitely a tough guy to like, but he wasn't the only Oakland star to have a tough World Series in 1988. Normally productive A's players (with more subtle personalities) like Mark McGwire (.059), Walt Weiss (.063), and Dennis Eckersley (0–1, 10.80) each contributed to the collapse. Somehow, though, you felt for them more.

Chicago Cubs/Leo Durocher
The 1969 Season

NATIONAL LEAGUE STANDINGS, SEPTEMBER 3, 1969

Team	W	L	PCT	GB
Chicago	84	53	.613	—
New York	77	56	.579	5

FINAL NATIONAL LEAGUE STANDINGS, 1969

Team	W	L	PCT	GB
New York	100	62	.617	—
Chicago	92	70	.568	8

The Cubs' last World Series championship was in 1908. Even those perrenial symbols of near-misses, the Boston Red Sox, can't boast such a championship drought. Of course, there have been years that the Cubs have come close, only to lose at the tail end of the season. 1969 was such a year.

The team had a devoted following that grew more and more excited as that fateful season wore on. Their Cubbies snagged first place in early April and hung onto it for nearly five months before they limped through an eight-game losing streak in early September and finally surrendered first place to the surging Miracle Mets.

September for the Cubs was a month of bad timing, bad luck, and just plain bad baseball. Fluky infield muffs, boneheaded pickoff attempts and a worn-out roster all took their toll. Furthermore, the Cubs would typically win a blowout game and follow up by getting swept in a doubleheader the next day. In fact, the Cubs were 13–17 in doubleheader play that season, compared to the Mets' 30–14 twinbill record.

Whose fault was all this? Fiery Chicago manager Leo Durocher was a frequent target. He was roundly criticized for his tactics. When Durocher's bullpen floundered, he overworked his starters, sometimes starting Fergie Jenkins and Ken Holtzman with only two days' rest. He overworked his regular hitters, too, and during the second half of the season, injuries sprang up all over the place. Ron Santo, Glenn Beckert, Don Kessinger, and Randy Hundley were all suffering from various injuries. But like Don Zimmer in 1978 (see chapter on the 1978 Red Sox), Durocher kept these beat-up guys in the lineup every day. As a result, run production plummeted, and in the crucial stretch from September 3rd to the 15th, Chicago lost eleven out of twelve games.

Meanwhile, the Mets, a 100–1 shot at the season's outset, were playing hot baseball, at one point winning 35 of 41. In the end, it wasn't even close; New York clinched the National League East division on September 23. At season's end, they stood a full eight games ahead of the ragged Cubs. "The best team that never won" had failed to win once again.

The Verdict

In responding to our goat survey, Alan Hoskins, sports columnist for the *Kansas City Kansan*, wrote, "Were the Cubs of 1969 'goats'? No. They did not lose the pennant that year; the Mets won it by taking 100 games, including 24 of their last 31." The Amazin' Mets, of course, were the ones responsible for that incredible streak and they were the ones who engineered the World Series championship against the tough Baltimore Orioles. Few baseball fans (Chicago natives not included) can argue that they didn't deserve it.

Joe Jackson

Chicago White Sox
"The Black Sox"
World Series *vs.* Cincinnati Reds
October 1–9, 1919

HITTERS

Name, position	1919 AVG	1919 WS AVG	1920 AVG
Happy Felsch, of	.275	.192	.338
Chick Gandil, 1b	.290	.233	Did not play
Joe Jackson, of	.351	.375	.382
Swede Risberg, ss	.256	.080	.266
Buck Weaver, 3b	.296	.324	.333

PITCHERS

Name	1919 ERA	1919 WS ERA	Lifetime ERA
Eddie Cicotte	1.82	2.91	2.38
Lefty Williams	2.64	6.61	3.13

During baseball's early years, gambling, cheating, and game fixing were as common as brush-back pitches and salty language. Yet no instance of chicanery is more famous or controversial than the Chicago White Sox' throwing of the 1919 World Series.

No doubt, the 1919 White Sox were a talented lot. The great Shoeless Joe Jackson, with a lifetime batting average of .356, ranks third on the all-time list in that department. Pitcher Ed Cicotte had five seasons with an ERA of under 2.00, winning 210 games in his career. Eddie Collins, Ray Schalk, and Red Faber made the Hall of Fame. And Buck Weaver was such a respected third baseman that even Ty Cobb wouldn't test him with a bunt. All of this talent made the White Sox far and away the year's most dominant team, and perhaps one of the greatest teams in baseball history. It is no wonder that the Sox were favored to beat the Cincinnati Reds in the World Series.

It was this favored position that prompted Chicago first baseman Chick Gandil to approach a Boston bookmaker and offer to throw the Series for $80,000. Gandil later enlisted the help of fellow teammates whom he thought were essential to the plan's success, men he was on friendly terms with. Eventually Gandil persuaded pitchers Ed Cicotte and Claude "Lefty" Williams, right fielder Jackson, shortstop Swede Risberg, center fielder Oscar "Happy" Felsch, and reserve infielder Fred McMullin to agree to do their best to lose the World Series on purpose. Third baseman Buck Weaver knew about their plan, but never agreed to participate.

When the Series got under way, shady rumors were already flying, and the play of the Sox did little to quell them, much less add subtlety to their intentions. Cincinnati won the best-of-nine series 5 games to 3. The only reason it was that close was because the conspiring Black Sox picked the sixth and seventh games of the Series to rebel against the gamblers, who had not yet handed over all the promised cash. The Series ended in the eighth game when threats of bodily harm from the gamblers put the rebels back in their place.

After such an apparent World Series upset, rumors continued with more fervor. Investigations were begun. As much as White Sox owner Charlie Comiskey tried to cover up the misdeeds of his star players, the truth soon emerged. Too many people had known about the fix from the start, and those who hadn't were able to figure it out by the shabby performance of key members of the heavily-favored Chicago squad.

The case eventually went to a grand jury in June of 1921. The eight key players were acquitted, yet baseball's commissioner, Judge Kenesaw Mountain Landis, still banned every one of them from baseball for life, stating, ". . . Regardless of the verdict of juries, no player who throws a ball game, no player that undertakes or promises to throw a ball game, no player that sits in conference with a bunch of crooked players and gamblers, where the ways and means of throwing a game are discussed and does not promptly tell his club about it, will ever play professional baseball!"

The Verdict

There are not many who dispute Judge Landis' decision concerning six of the eight "Black Sox." Cicotte, Williams, Felch, Risberg, Gandil, and McMullin purposely took part in the scandal, blatantly threw games, and took money for their services. This behavior apparently didn't stop at the 1919 World Series; these characters later threw more games in 1920, including three against Cleveland in an effort to keep the pennant race close. They made no attempt to conceal what they were doing and, if their behavior in 1920 indicates, they had no remorse and no intentions of halting their dishonest mode of play. Granted, the lifetime ban was extreme, but so was the fixing of baseball games. If these players were made an example of, they have no one to blame but themselves for participating in activities that qualified them to be examples.

However, the same standards are usually not used when considering the cases of Shoeless Joe Jackson and Buck Weaver. While both knew of the intentions of their teammates, they gave World Series perfomances that were consistent with their typical outstanding play. At .375, Jackson's batting average in the Series was a full 24 points *higher* than his regular season's. Similarly, Weaver improved his season average 28 points in the World Series. In addition, both Jackson and Weaver improved over the course of the 1920 season (see accompanying chart).

While Jackson received $5,000 as a result of the fix, he was considered a simple man who never fully understood the whole situation. With wads of cash waved in front of his face, it is argued, he went along with the plans of his friends, but couldn't follow through once he stepped onto the playing field. Weaver, on the other hand, never took any money and never even agreed to participate in the fix; his downfall came from the fact that he was present at two of the conspirators' meetings and declined to warn anyone about their plans.

Of the eight banned players, only Jackson and Weaver didn't deserve to wear the goat horns, just as they didn't deserve to be banned from baseball for life. They were guilty of poor judgement, not tarnishing the game of baseball; the same cannot be said of their teammates.

Roger Clemens

Pitcher
Boston Red Sox
American League Playoffs *vs.* Oakland A's
October 10, 1990

YEAR	TEAM	W	L	G	GS	IP	H	BB	SO	ERA
1984	Red Sox	9	4	21	20	133	146	29	126	4.33
1985	Red Sox	7	5	15	15	98	83	37	74	3.31
1986	Red Sox	24	4	33	33	254	179	67	238	2.48
1987	Red Sox	20	9	36	36	282	248	83	256	2.97
1988	Red Sox	18	12	35	35	264	217	62	291	2.93
1989	Red Sox	17	11	35	35	253	215	93	230	3.13
1990	Red Sox	21	6	31	31	228	193	54	209	1.93
1991	Red Sox	18	10	35	35	271	219	65	241	2.62
	CAREER TOTALS	134	61	241	240	1783	1500	460	1665	2.85

This much is clear. Roger Clemens, trailing 1–0 with his team facing elimination at the hands of the Oakland A's, said *something* distinctive to plate umpire Terry Cooney during the second inning of the fourth game of the 1990 American League Championship Series. Just what it was the three-time Cy Young award-winner came up with was not apparent at the time. But whatever it was, he said it after shaking his head at a called ball four. And whatever it was, Cooney didn't like it at all.

To the contrary, Cooney, a formidable presence who had spent time as a prison guard in his pre-umpiring days, tossed Clemens out of the game without hesitation. The Sox got little more than an inning out of their top starter in the biggest single game of the year. Oakland ended up winning, 3–1, behind the tough Dave Stewart—taking their third pennant in as many years.

So what happened? Well, extensive review of the videotape has yielded the following (admittedly sketchy) transcription of the exchange between pitcher and umpire. Let's listen in.

> *Cooney:* Ball four! (Oakland second baseman Willie Randolph trots to first.)
>
> *Clemens (Shaking his head):* Gosh, ump, I sure must have missed my Wheaties this morning. Heaven only knows what I'll do next. And I usually have such exceptional control! Isn't that just like me to make such a golldarned mess of things?
>
> *Cooney:* There, there, Roger. You're too hard on yourself. Take it from me.

> *Clemens:* Heck and double-heck, ump. I guess you're right. I wish I could have some time to collect myself.
>
> *Cooney:* That can certainly be arranged, Roger. Why don't you head back into the clubhouse and take a seat?
>
> *Clemens:* Shoot! Why not?

Actually, our transcription may be off by a word or two. Interviews with players from both sides actually attributed the following gems to Clemens in reaction to Cooney:

> *"Why don't you take your mask off if you want to talk to me?"*
>
> *"I'm not shaking my (expletive) head at you. If you want to talk to me, take your mask off."*
>
> *"Then just keep your (expletive) mask on and call the (expletive) game."*
>
> *"Get your (expletive) ass behind the plate right now."*
>
> *"You gutless (expletive)."*

Well. Whatever Clemens said, it probably wasn't material you're likely to hear covered in a Dale Carnegie course on winning friends and influencing people. And, more to the point, it hurt the Red Sox in a big way. First and foremost, of course, they lost Clemens. Additionally, they lost a good deal of momentum in a crucial game. And then there was the matter of second baseman Marty Barrett, who threw two water coolers and a trash bin full of bubble gum and sunflower seeds onto the field in protest of Cooney's call. He got the heave-ho, as well.

It was not a graceful inning.

The game as a whole was a truly ugly end to a promising season for the Red Sox. We will probably never know how the contest might have turned out had Roger kept his cool, but it's safe to say that Boston was outclassed from the first game to (especially) the last in this series. The Rocket's main accomplishment on this day was overestimating the bounds his superstar status accorded him. ("We cannot rewrite the rule book for Roger Clemens," umpire Jim Evans pointed out after the game.) His miscalculation cost his team the game—but it cost the game itself something, too.

An unpleasant episode for all concerned.

The Verdict

Many argued that umpire Cooney acted too hastily in ejecting Clemens from this game, but the league disagreed—and so did a lot of major league players. Roger went over the line by a fair distance and got the result he—if not the fans of New England—deserved.

Early Wynn

Cleveland Indians

World Series *vs.* New York Giants
September 29 - October 2, 1954

1954 REGULAR SEASON

TEAM	W	L	PCT	R	H	AVG	ERA
Cleveland A.L.	111	43	.721	746	1368	.262	2.78
New York N.L.	97	57	.630	732	1386	.264	3.09

1954 WORLD SERIES

TEAM	W	L	PCT	R	H	AVG	ERA
Cleveland A.L.	0	4	.000	9	26	.190	4.84
New York N.L.	4	0	1.000	21	33	.254	1.46

They've had a tough time of it through the years: a handful of pennants, only two world championships in their 90-year history, and not a single winning season since divisional play began in 1969. But in the summer of 1954, the Cleveland Indians were sitting on top of the world. Winning 111 games—an American League record, and second in the majors only to the 1906 Cubs' 116 victories—the Indians, it seemed, simply couldn't lose.

Cleveland surely had fine hitters, boasting moderate power from Larry Doby (32 homers) and Al Rosen (24 homers), but it was pitching that spelled their success that year. Bob Lemon, Early Wynn, and Mike Garcia won a total of 65 games. Art Houtteman went 15–7 while an aging but still effective Bob Feller was 13–3. Cleveland pitching allowed only 504 runs that year, tops in the majors. The team's earned run average was a ridiculously low 2.78, also tops.

While the Indians were shutting opponents out, the New York Yankees were having their own great season. It was the only season Casey Stengel's Yankees would win more than 100 games. They won 103 and led the American League in every major hitting category, but still couldn't win the pennant. Cleveland's untouchable pitching proved the difference, as the Indians maintained a comfortable eight-game lead over the Yanks through September and into the season's end.

Over in the National League, Leo Durocher piloted the New York Giants to a solid 97–57 first-place finish. Led by a promising young center fielder named Willie Mays (.345 average with 41 homers), the Giants also featured Don "Mandrake the Magician" Mueller (.342) and rock-solid shortstop Al Dark. The Giants' pitching was adequate, but nothing to write home about. John Antonelli won 21 and legendary reliever Hoyt Wilhelm sported a nifty 2.11 ERA, but that was about it.

Certainly the Giants were a worthy bunch, but they were also heavy underdogs when it came to challenging the mighty Indians at World Series time. At season's end, nine out of every ten sportswriters predicted doom for Durocher's club.

Interestingly, however, the Indians had been thrashed several times by the Giants during spring training. Monte Irvin remembered his team's confidence going into the Series; "We used to play [the Indians] in the spring and beat them regularly. They had good power and outstanding pitching, but their defense wasn't too good and they didn't have much speed."

The Series got under way in New York's famed Polo Grounds. Cleveland jumped on the board first for a 2–0 lead in the first inning of Game 1, but the Giants tied it up in the bottom of the third. Pitchers Bob Lemon and Sal Maglie settled down for a while, but Cleveland looked to break things open in the top of the eighth. With men on first and second, Vic Wertz came to bat and hit a tremendous blast to deep center. The hit would have easily been a homer in a smaller park, but the immense Polo Grounds swallowed it up.

What happened next is generally acknowledged as the greatest catch in World Series history. Willie Mays came out of nowhere and somehow caught the ball over his shoulder, spun around and fired it back. He would later say he knew he had it the whole time. Left fielder Monte Irvin had a different view, admitting he had given up on the ball and was hoping to hold Wertz to a triple. In any event, Mays' spectacular catch took the wind out of Cleveland's sails—permanently.

The Indians lost Game 1 in the bottom of the ninth on a pinch-homer by Dusty Rhodes, and it was downhill for Cleveland from there. They dropped the final three games by scores of 3–1, 6–2, and 7–4 for a humiliating, inexplicable sweep. The team that had won 111 games in the regular season couldn't manage a single victory against the crafty Giants.

The Verdict

Could the New York Giants actually have been the better team? In the late 40's and early 50's, the New York Yankees had dominated the American League for so long that a kind of apathy had developed among other A.L. ballclubs. There were truly horrible teams such as the Philadelphia A's and Baltimore Orioles, and there were very good teams like the Indians, Yankees, and Chicago White Sox. But there *weren't* many middle-of-the-road teams to add balance. In fact, in 1954 there weren't *any* A.L teams with a winning percentage between .450 and .610!

Furthermore, some American League teams of this period were still hesitant to sign black players. By 1954, all but one National League team were racially integrated, while the American League still had three teams following an "all-white" policy. This outdated practice left the more progressive National League with a large pool of fresh talent from which to build teams.

These two factors could lead to a conclusion not widely held in 1954: that the Indians were a very good team playing in a less competitive league, while the New York Giants were a superior team playing in a far more competitive league.

Willie Davis
Outfield
Los Angeles Dodgers
World Series *vs*. Baltimore Orioles
October 6, 1966

CAREER HIGHLIGHTS

YEAR	TEAM	AVG	G	AB	R	H	2B	3B	HR	RBI
1962	Dodgers	.285	157	600	103	171	18	10	21	85
1966	Dodgers	.284	153	624	74	177	31	6	11	61
1969	Dodgers	.311	129	498	66	155	23	8	11	59
1970	Dodgers	.305	146	593	92	181	23	16	8	93
1971	Dodgers	.309	158	641	84	198	33	10	10	74
1972	Dodgers	.289	149	615	81	178	22	7	19	79
1973	Dodgers	.285	152	599	82	171	29	9	16	77
1974	Expos	.295	153	611	86	180	27	9	12	89
	CAREER TOTALS	.279	2429	9174	1217	2561	395	138	182	1053

The '66 Fall Classic was an odd affair. The Baltimore Orioles swept the Los Angeles Dodgers in four games, but hit only .200 as a team (the lowest World Series average by a sweeper). The lackluster Dodgers were even worse, hitting .142, scoring only two runs, and being shut out in the final three games! However, the fact that Sandy Koufax made his last professional appearance—losing to 20-year-old prodigy Jim Palmer in the now-legendary Game 2—did help keep fans' interest up.

As numbingly cold as the Dodgers were as a team, it's centerfielder Willie Davis who is remembered as one of the Series' coldest players. He contributed only one hit in 16 at bats for an .063 average—pretty much par for the Dodger course. But he also made three errors in the fifth inning of Game 2 which, much to the delight of the Orioles, led to three unearned runs.

It was a scoreless game going into the top of the fifth inning in Los Angeles. Both the youngster Palmer and the veteran Koufax had good stuff. Then, with one out and Oriole Boog Powell at first, Paul Blair hit a high fly to center. The late afternoon sun was now peeking over the stadium roof and the L.A. smog had created a nasty glare for Willie Davis to fight. He lost the battle, dropped the ball, and allowed Powell to go to third and Blair to go to second. Andy Etchebarren came to bat and created another solar eclipse with the baseball when he popped to center. Again, Willie lost the ball. Powell chugged home and Blair raced toward third. Davis then picked up the ball and, in a futile attempt to nail the swift Blair at third, whipped it right into the Dodger dugout. Blair scored and Davis was booed. Before the hellish inning was over, the Orioles would add a third unearned run.

In the sixth inning, Davis had yet another fielding problem when he and right fielder Ron Fairly avoided a collision by letting Frank Robinson's pop fly fall between them for a three-base error. The muff was attributed to Fairly, but easily could have been pinned on Davis for his fourth error of the game. Perhaps the official scorer felt Davis had suffered enough.

When the dust had settled, the Dodgers had committed a total of six errors in the game. Baltimore took full advantage and won the game 6–0 to take a two-games-to-none lead in the Series. After the sloppy game, Davis said, "I don't feel either [of the balls lost in the sun] should have been an error, although, of course, the throw was. I lost sight of both balls on their way down."

Oriole manager Hank Bauer agreed with Davis, saying at the time, "If the ball is right in the sun, you're blind. If it's to the edge of the sun, you have a chance."

The next day, the *New York Times* ran headlines that said, "Goathood Looms for Willie Davis." As with Johnny Pesky in 1946 (see chapter on Pesky), the papers needed only to mention the word "goat" in connection with Davis, and poor Willie's fate was sealed.

The Dodgers went down meekly in Games 3 and 4, losing two consecutive 1–0 shutouts and setting a Series record for going thirty-three consecutive innings without scoring a single run.

The Verdict

Davis committed a record three errors in one inning of a World Series game. Admittedly, that sounds pretty bad; and it is bad if those three errors lost the game. But Davis alone lost neither Game 2 nor the Series for the Dodgers. First of all, two of his errors were fly balls clearly lost in the sun. These balls would have required ESP to catch. Secondly, the Dodgers provided no offensive support for Sandy Koufax's fine outing—they couldn't touch Jim Palmer all day, squeaking out only four hits and not scoring at all. Davis could have committed a hundred errors or none at all in Game 2 and it wouldn't have affected the outcome of Palmer's shutout. If any goat trophy should be awarded for the 1966 World Series, it should go to the Dodgers' bats.

Don Denkinger

Umpire
American League
World Series
Kansas City Royals *vs*. St. Louis Cardinals
October 26, 1985

The scrappy Kansas City Royals barely managed to claw their way into the 1985 World Series. Clinching their division by just one game with only 91 wins, they came back from a 3 games to 1 deficit against the Blue Jays in the American League Playoffs. Stiff competition awaited in the form of the St. Louis Cardinals for the "All-Missouri" World Series. The heavily favored Cardinals had won 101 games and led the league in most major offensive categories, including an astonishing 314 stolen bases.

From the start, the Series looked to be a pitchers' duel. The Cards were able to take the first two games in Kansas City with a measly total of seven runs and thirteen hits. The Series moved to St. Louis, where the Royals won Game 3 behind the pitching of Bret Saberhagen, who would later be awarded the A.L. Cy Young Award.

After shutting out the Royals 3–0 in Game 4, the Cards were up three games to one and poised to walk away with their second championship in four years. But Danny Jackson cooled St. Louis off, tossing a five-hitter to make it three games to two.

At this point, neither team was doing much hitting. And the speedy Cards had only stolen two bases—an extremely low number for them. Sports columnists were already dubbing it "The Most Boring World Series Ever." This would all change in the eighth inning of Game 6.

On October 26, Danny Cox took the mound for St. Louis against Charlie Leibrandt, whose career was marked by an above-average number of tough losses. "The Most Boring World Series Ever" continued as such, with both pitchers holding their opponents scoreless for seven innings.

But with two out in the top of the eighth inning, the Cards got two men on. Utility man Brian Harper was sent in to pinch hit for Cox. Harper, a .250 lifetime hitter, delivered a bloop hit, knocking in the game's first run and bringing his team to the brink of victory.

The bottom of the ninth arrived, and the anxious Cards were three outs away from champagne showers. Pinch hitter Jorge Orta stepped up to the plate and quickly got in the hole 0–2. On the third pitch he reached out and rolled the ball in between first baseman Jack Clark and Todd Worrell, the new St. Louis pitcher. Clark picked it up and flipped it to the covering Worrell to beat Orta.

At least that's how it looked on the video replays. But first base ump Don Denkinger saw it differently and called Orta safe. St. Louis manager Whitey Herzog burst onto the field and screamed until he was blue, but the call stood and the Royals caught a huge break.

Denkinger's bad call was the rallying cry for the Royals and the choke signal for the Cardinals. The next batter, Steve Balboni, popped up in foul territory on the first base side. Inexplicably, Clark didn't catch the ball. Balboni then hit a single. At this point, then, there should have been two outs with nobody on—instead there were no outs with two on.

After a force out, a passed ball, an intentional walk, and a broken-bat bloop single by Dane Iorg, the Royals had set aside any notion that this was a boring World Series. They triumphed 2–1 to tie the series and force a final, deciding game. St. Louis fans bristled at the thought. If only Denkinger had made the right call . . . .

As it turned out, Game 7 was a joke. The previous game had knocked the wind out of St. Louis and they crumbled under the Royals' 11-run, 14-hit attack. Kansas City had emerged from the depths of a three-games-to-one deficit to win the first World Series in the franchise's history—with a little help from Don Denkinger.

The Verdict

Denkinger got the Royals going with
his blatantly muffed call in Game 6.
Jack Clark kept the Kansas City ball
rolling by spacing out immediately
afterwards. Together, they handed the
Royals the pivotal Game 6. But it
isn't Clark you'll hear St. Louis fans
howling about; the ump made a much
easier target.

Leon Durham
First Base
Chicago Cubs
National League Playoffs *vs.* San Diego Padres
October 7, 1984

YEAR	TEAM	AVG	G	AB	R	H	2B	3B	HR	RBI
1980	Cardinals	.271	96	303	42	82	15	4	8	42
1981	Cubs	.290	87	328	42	95	14	6	10	35
1982	Cubs	.312	148	539	84	168	33	7	22	90
1983	Cubs	.258	100	337	58	87	18	8	12	55
1984	Cubs	.279	137	473	86	132	30	4	23	96
1985	Cubs	.282	153	542	58	153	32	2	21	75
1986	Cubs	.262	141	484	66	127	18	7	20	65
1987	Cubs	.273	131	439	70	120	22	1	27	63
1988	Cubs	.219	24	73	10	16	6	1	3	6
1988	Reds	.216	21	51	4	11	3	0	1	2
1989	Cardinals	.056	29	18	2	1	1	0	0	1
	CAREER TOTALS	.277	1067	3587	522	992	192	40	147	530

In 1984, the Chicago Cubs, who hadn't won a pennant since 1945 or a World Series since 1908, seemed to be battling not only the Padres in this playoff series, but also their own history. They lost to both.

When it was all said and done, the Padres had taken the series, 3 games to 2, overcoming the Cubs' two-game advantage to win the last three at home. As is usually the case after such a defeat, a search was begun for what went wrong, and who was to blame.

Most eyes turned to the fifth game, and to Cub first baseman Leon Durham. Durham had started out the game as the would-be hero, blasting a two-run homer in the first to give Chicago an early lead. They added another run with Jody Davis' solo homer in the second. Rick Sutcliffe was pitching shutout ball. Everything was falling into place for the Cubs; their first pennant in 39 years was just a few innings away.

In the sixth, Sutcliffe gave up two San Diego runs. Then, with his team clinging to a 3–2 lead in the seventh, he walked Carmelo Martinez, who advanced to second on a sacrifice bunt. With Martinez in scoring position, Durham let a grounder slip under his glove, and suddenly the game was tied at three.

It may have been Durham's worst moment, but there was more in store for Chicago. Sutcliffe thought he was finally out of the inning when he got Padre Tony Gwynn to hit a grounder for what looked like an easy double play. But the ball took a nasty bounce off the hard San Diego infield and jetted past second baseman Ryne Sandberg. It found its way all the way to the fence. Gwynn had himself a two-run double, took third on the throw home, and the score stood at 5–3.

If that wasn't enough to deflate the Cubs, Steve Garvey's bat was. Garvey had been red hot throughout the series, batting .400 with eight hits and belting a two-run game-winning homer in the bottom of the ninth in Game 4. With first base vacant, Cubs' manager Jim Frey opted to pitch to Garvey. Big mistake. Garvey cracked a base hit to boost the Padre lead to 6–3 and cap the San Diego comeback. They were on their way to the World Series. The 1984 Cubs were left, as were their predecessors, pondering could-have-beens.

The Verdict

Although Leon Durham is the guy whose error allowed the Padres to get into the game and gain momentum, he's not the only goat wearing a Cubs uniform. If Durham's perceived goat status is rooted in the idea that his error started this chain of events, that notion deserves a second look. There were a few errors and bad breaks that alone were not enough to cost the game, but in combination were deadly: the two runs Sutcliffe gave up in the sixth, the key walk in the seventh, Durham's error, Gwynn's fluke bad-hop double, and Garvey's clutch single.

For a team with such a long dry spell to come so close, a scapegoat might have been what Chicago needed to ease the pain. But if truth be told, either the team as a whole deserves the horns, or no one at all. As Cub centerfielder Bob Dernier said after the game, "We lost this one as a team."

Jerry Dybzinski
Shortstop
Chicago White Sox
American League Playoffs *vs.* Baltimore Orioles
October 8, 1983

YEAR	TEAM	AVG	G	AB	R	H	2B	3B	HR	RBI
1980	Indians	.230	114	248	32	57	11	1	1	23
1981	Indians	.298	48	57	10	17	0	0	0	6
1982	Indians	.231	80	212	19	49	6	2	0	22
1983	White Sox	.230	127	256	30	59	10	1	1	32
1984	White Sox	.235	94	132	17	31	5	1	1	10
1985	Pirates	.000	5	4	0	0	0	0	0	0
	CAREER TOTALS	.234	468	909	108	213	32	5	3	93

"I felt like a beached whale out there." So said Chicago White Sox utility man Jerry Dybzinski after he found himself trapped between second and third in a do-or-die 1983 playoff game against the Baltimore Orioles. Beached whale indeed—he and the rest of his team.

The White Sox got off on the right foot, winning the first game of the best-of-five American League Playoffs at Baltimore's Memorial Stadium, 2–1. But Baltimore rookie Mike Boddicker pitched a masterful 4–0 shutout in Game 2 to tie the series. The ice-cold Sox would score only one more run in the entire series—that one coming in the Oriole's 11–1 Game 3 blowout.

With Baltimore leading the series two games to one, the Chisox still had a chance for salvation going into Game 4. In front of their home crowd, they had Britt Burns on the mound. Holding the Orioles scoreless, Burns was delivering a career performance. But the White Sox were stranding runners left and right.

In the bottom of the seventh inning, Dybzinski came to bat with no outs and runners on first and second. Chicago manager Tony LaRussa gave him specific instructions to sacrifice the runners over, but Dybzinski's bunt was bad and Oriole catcher Rick Dempsey easily nailed the runner at third. Now there was one out with Vance Law on second and Dybzinski on first. Jose Cruz stepped up and rapped a solid single to left. Dybzinski motored around second and headed towards third.

There was only one problem. Dybzinski was looking down as he approached third. If he had been looking up, he would have seen Law standing on the base. Dybzinski tried to scamper back to second but got caught in a rundown. Law tried to score but was tagged out.

The inning ended and the score was still 0–0. The Chisox hit three singles to the outfield in one inning and somehow failed to score. Dybzinski's baserunning mistake loomed larger as the game wore on.

Britt Burns did a tremendous job for Chicago, pitching nine and a third scoreless innings before yielding a solo home run to Tito Landrum in the top of the tenth. Landrum's blast was all the Orioles needed. They wound up winning the game 3–0, and snagged the A.L. pennant. A week later they would beat the Philadelphia Phillies in the World Series.

As the Orioles celebrated their victory and the White Sox reflected on their loss, Dybzinski's running blunder was the big topic of conversation. But he handled his sudden goathood with remarkable class. He said at the time, "A lot's going to be written and said, but I'm going to be no worse for wear. I know I can run the bases. I know I can bunt. If I can handle this, it'll make me better for it." A reporter, amazed at how well Dybzinski was taking the whole situation, asked him if he learned how to handle things this well from his dad. Jerry managed a subdued chuckle, saying, "I don't think my father ever got caught between second and third."

The Verdict

Dybzinski is surely guilty as charged, but give him some credit for at least wearing the goat horns gracefully. Consider, too, the misdeeds of the following Chisox players: pitcher Richard Dotson, who gave up six earned runs in five innings during Game 3; designated hitter Greg Luzinski, who struck out five times and went 2-for-15 in the series; and outfielder Rudy Law who took a called strike three with two outs in the bottom of the ninth and the winning run at third.

Dennis Eckersley
Pitcher
Oakland Athletics
World Series *vs*. Los Angeles Dodgers
October 15, 1988

CAREER HIGHLIGHTS

YEAR	TEAM	W	L	SV	G	GS	IP	H	BB	SO	ERA
1975	Indians	13	7	2	34	24	187	147	90	152	2.60
1977	Indians	14	13	0	33	33	247	214	54	191	3.53
1978	Red Sox	20	8	0	35	35	268	258	71	162	2.99
1979	Red Sox	17	10	0	33	33	247	234	59	150	2.99
1981	Red Sox	9	8	0	23	23	154	160	35	79	4.27
1982	Red Sox	13	13	0	33	33	224	228	43	127	3.74
1984	Cubs	10	8	0	24	24	160	152	36	81	3.04
1985	Cubs	11	7	0	25	25	169	145	19	117	3.09
1988	A's	4	2	45	60	0	73	52	11	70	2.34
1989	A's	4	0	33	51	0	58	32	3	55	1.55
1990	A's	4	2	48	63	0	73	41	4	73	0.61
1991	A's	5	4	43	67	0	76	60	9	87	2.96
CAREER TOTALS		174	144	188	671	361	2891	2685	668	2025	3.47

The story is something right out of the film *The Natural.* An ailing Kirk Gibson, his leg injuries so serious he has spent the entire game in the training room, is called to the plate to pinch hit in the bottom of the ninth of Game 1 of the 1988 World Series. Two out; one on; Gibson's team, the Dodgers, down by a run against the mighty Oakland Athletics, winners of 104 games during the regular season. Gibson steps—limps—to the plate to face baseball's premier stopper . . . then belts a game-winning homer and, once he has trotted joyously but unsteadily around the bases, scores the winning run. The hometown crowd goes mad.

Nice story. Unless you're Dennis Eckersley, the man who yielded the homer.

Implausibly enough, the 1988 Series ended up going the Dodgers' way, and dissecters of the championship games keep coming back to that critical confrontation, Eckersley against Gibson in Game 1. Hadn't it set the stage somehow? Hadn't that one at-bat summed up the entire never-say-die Los Angeles season? Hadn't the home run given the underdog Dodgers an emotional boost sufficient to allow them to overcome, in only five games, a roster considered by most experts to be the best since Cincinnati's Big Red Machine of the seventies?

Put bluntly, most fans—and most in the national media—had considered the Athletics a sure thing against the Dodgers. Oakland hadn't come through, and in large measure, it was argued, it was because Eckersley had been unable to retire a man who was barely able to walk to the plate.

It's hard to put into words how dominant Eckersley had been over the course of the season, but a few of the Eck's statistics from that year will serve to illustrate the point. The Oakland stopper logged a league-leading 45 saves, struck out nearly seven times as many people as he walked, and posted an ERA of 2.34. 1988 was the year Eckersley turned around, having overcome a nasty batch of personal problems and established himself as the American League's top relief pitcher after a twelve-year career as a starter. That Eckersley should conclude his banner year with a Series ERA of 10.80 and the most agonizing blown save of the season must have been hard for him—and Oakland partisans—to swallow.

Some curious parallels emerge, however, between Eckersley's infamous gopher ball in the 1988 Series and Babe Ruth's basestealing antics in the 1926 classic. (See Ruth's chapter.) The Bambino's ill-fated attempt to steal second with two outs in the ninth in the deciding game cost his team a world championship that went instead to the St. Louis Cardinals. And Eckersley yielded a game-winning home run that set the stage for his team's defeat to a Dodger team that was, on paper, markedly inferior to Oakland. But what a difference a year makes! In the following seasons, each player posted downright surreal numbers en route to his team's World Series sweep. The Babe, of course, blasted 60 home runs in 1927 and led the Yankees to a four-game annihilation of the Pirates; Eckersley's 1989 season featured 55 strikeouts against only three walks, 33 saves, and an ERA of 1.56. More to the point, Eck's Athletics dismantled crosstown rivals San Francisco in four games.

The Verdict

The glories of the following season not-withstanding, Eckersley's job in Game 1 of the '88 Series eventually boiled down to this: Get Kirk Gibson to limp back to the bench with his bat in his hands. Instead, Gibson limped around the bases and into the history books. Hang the horns on the Eck for this one.

Charlie O. Finley

Charlie O. Finley, Owner and
Mike Andrews, 2nd Base
Oakland Athletics
World Series *vs.* New York Mets
October 14, 1973

MIKE ANDREWS

YEAR	TEAM	AVG	G	AB	R	H	2B	3B	HR	RBI
1966	Red Sox	.167	5	18	1	3	0	0	0	0
1967	Red Sox	.263	142	494	79	130	20	0	8	40
1968	Red Sox	.271	147	536	77	145	22	1	7	45
1969	Red Sox	.293	121	464	79	136	26	2	15	59
1970	Red Sox	.253	151	589	91	149	28	1	17	65
1971	White Sox	.282	109	330	45	93	16	0	12	47
1972	White Sox	.220	148	505	58	111	18	0	7	50
1973	White Sox	.201	52	159	10	32	9	0	0	10
1973	A's	.190	18	21	1	4	1	0	0	0
	CAREER TOTALS	.258	893	3116	441	803	140	4	66	316

What on earth does it mean when sportswriters nominate not only a player but the team owner as "co-goats"? It means you've landed smack in the middle of the Oakland A's dynasty of the early '70's. The Oakland squads of '72, '73, and '74 won three consecutive world championships despite poor attendance, day-glo uniforms, and less-than-perfect team chemistry. The attendance problems had a lot to do with a competing outfit in nearby Candlestick Park; the rest of the league eventually got used to the uniforms. However, the team's infighting, frequent managerial changes, and notoriously bad press were all directly or indirectly traceable to the consistently high-handed personnel tactics of owner Charlie Finley. Finley's run-in with backup infielder Mike Andrews during the '73 Series showed the owner in his worst light.

In Game 2 of that fall classic, the Mets and A's were tied 6–6 going into the twelfth inning. The game was chugging along into its fourth hour. In the top of the inning, the New Yorkers scored four runs, three of which resulted when Andrews, a late-inning replacement, booted two grounders in a row. Oakland squeezed across a run in the bottom of the inning, but the final score was 10–7, Mets. The Series was even at a game apiece.

Andrews knew his errors had been costly ones, and that they had lost the A's a game. His teammates, however, held nothing against him and urged him to maintain an upbeat attitude; the Series wasn't over yet. But as far as Finley was concerned, it was over—for Andrews.

Immediately after that second game, Charlie O. ordered that Andrews be examined by team physician Harry R. Walker, who performed what could charitably be described as a cursory examination. Walker declared that Andrews had seriously injured his shoulder, although Mike insisted to the doctor that he felt fine.

Never one to suffer a hired hand who couldn't take a hint, Finley later summoned the infielder to his office for a personal meeting. There the owner demanded that Andrews sign a statement acknowledging that he was injured and unable to play. (This was apparently a misguided attempt to open up another roster spot for Oakland's remaining Series games.) Still Andrews resisted. He related the following conversation to a *New York Times* reporter:

Andrews: "You want me to lie?"

Finley: "No."

Andrews: "How else do you explain it?"

Finley: "You want to help the ball club?"

Andrews: "Yes, but not this way."

After lengthy bullying, Andrews gave in and signed. Finley sent him home to Massachusetts. The whole arrangement was declared void in short order, however, when Commissioner Bowie Kuhn got wind of Finley's machinations. Andrews eventually rejoined the team in New York. His teammates, who had worn black armbands on their uniforms in protest during his absence, gave him an enthusiastic welcome back.

Andrews batted only once more in the Series, grounding out—although he received a standing ovation on taking his place in the batter's box. The A's went on to win the Finley-marred Series, 4 games to 3.

The Verdict

Don't let his two costly errors fool you; Andrews wasn't the real goat here. That honor goes to Finley, who proved that if you're petty and shortsighted enough, you can find a way to tarnish even a world championship season.

Harry Frazee
Owner
Boston Red Sox
1916–1923

BOSTON RED SOX WITH BABE RUTH AS A MEMBER (1914–1919):
- Wins: 514
- Losses: 359
- Percentage: .589
- Number of pennants: 3
- Number of World Championships: 3
- Highest winning percentage: .669 in 1915
- Lowest winning percentage: .482 in 1919

BOSTON RED SOX AFTER HARRY FRAZEE SOLD BABE RUTH (1920–1935):
- Wins: 969
- Losses: 1478
- Percentage: .396
- Number of pennants: 0
- Number of World Championships: 0
- Highest winning percentage: .510 in 1935
- Lowest winning percentage: .279 in 1932

(Stats are during Babe Ruth's active career)

It's the tail end of 1919. A young fellow named George Herman Ruth just demolished the major league record for home runs in a season. You own Ruth's baseball contract. You also own the dominant team in baseball—a team that has taken four out of the last eight World Series and is poised to win a fifth in the coming season. What's your move?

If you're Harry Frazee, obviously you sell this Ruth character to the New York Yankees for cash and watch your team venture down to the musty American League basement for a twenty-year hibernation.

This is exactly what Frazee, owner of the Boston Red Sox, did. Boston fans call Frazee's ridiculous move "the beginning of life with the Red Sox". *Boston Globe* columnist Dan Shaughnessy calls it "The Curse of the Bambino" and wrote an entire book on it. Call it what you will. The facts are that in the seventy-plus years since Frazee sold Babe Ruth, the Red Sox have won four division titles, four pennants, and no World Series.

In 1919, Frazee was having trouble making ends meet. He had purchased the mighty Red Sox club three years earlier from New Yorker Joe Lannin. Even though the Sox were immensely popular and successful, Frazee began to miss payments. It seems he was pouring more money into financing Broadway musical productions than he was into Lannin's bank account. It got to the point where Frazee considered offering his superstar pitcher/outfielder Babe Ruth up for sale to raise some cash.

Negotiations began. Rumors swept through Boston. At a January 5, 1920 news conference, Frazee announced that he had just completed a deal sending George Herman Ruth to the New York Yankees for $100,000 cash as well as a $300,000 loan. Red Sox fans were stunned. How could Harry

Frazee get rid of baseball's premier pitcher and new home run king? And to give him to the rival Yankees without getting any players in return was a double blow.

Frazee carefully skirted the issue of his Broadway musical projects by making it sound like Ruth was ruining the team. He told the press that Ruth had gotten out of control "... and the Boston club can no longer put up with his eccentricities ... While Ruth is undoubtedly the greatest hitter the game has ever seen, he is likewise one of the most selfish and inconsiderate men ever to put on a baseball uniform."

Let's see. He's 24, hits like a madman, owns an ERA in the low 2.00's, and led his team to several championship seasons. Sounds pretty good. Oh, but wait. He's inconsiderate—better sell him to the Yanks. They deserve all the head cases.

Mr. Frazee did not stop at selling Ruth. Over the next several years, he continued to generate cash for his Broadway musicals by selling star players to the Yankees. Waite Hoyt, Joe Dugan, Herb Pennock, and Everett Scott all became Yankee greats after being dumped by Frazee.

In 1923, Frazee bailed out of his baseball responsibilities and sold the team. But his haphazard sale of players had taken its toll. The Sox were crippled for decades.

At least Frazee finally had a hit with *No No, Nanette.*

The Verdict

It is hard not to notice that this book profiles a dispropor-
tionately large number of goats affiliated with the Boston
Red Sox. Several hundred sportswriters from around the
country (less than ten of whom were from greater Boston) selected the goats in this book. There is simply
something about the Red Sox, something . . . terrifying.
In any case, one look at the Babe's statistics safely
secures Harry Frazee the distinction of the grandaddy of
all Red Sox goats. Whether or not selling the Babe to the
dreaded Yankees brought on a curse is a matter of personal
opinion. But the magnitude of the loss to the fans of
New England is indisputable.

Tom Lasorda

Manager, Los Angeles Dodgers
National League Playoffs *vs.* St. Louis Cardinals
October 16, 1985

MANAGERIAL HIGHLIGHTS

YEAR	TEAM	W	L	Pct.	Standing
1976	Dodgers	2	2	.500	2
1977	Dodgers	98	64	.605	1
1978	Dodgers	95	67	.586	1
1980	Dodgers	92	71	.564	2
1981A	Dodgers	36	21	.632	1
1981B	Dodgers	27	26	.509	4
1982	Dodgers	88	74	.543	2
1983	Dodgers	91	71	.562	1
1985	Dodgers	95	67	.586	1
1988	Dodgers	94	67	.584	1
1990	Dodgers	86	76	.531	2
1991	Dodgers	93	69	.574	2
CAREER TOTALS		1278	1102	.537	

Tommy Lasorda started an avalanche of second-guessing when he ordered Tom Niedenfuer to pitch to Cardinal slugger Jack Clark in the ninth inning of a pennant-deciding game.

Since taking over the Dodger helm at the end of the 1976 season, Lasorda has piled up four pennants and two world championships and has developed a reputation of steadiness and harmony with his players. He is also known as somewhat of a character, hawking weight-loss products on TV and babbling on and on about trivial but entertaining subjects in interviews. He's well-liked by his players and employers alike and is generally known as a baseball "good guy."

In the 1985 National League playoffs, however, Lasorda hit his managerial low point when he made an extremely poor tactical decision. The Cardinals were up three games to two in the series and needed just one victory to take the pennant. But the Dodgers held a 4–1 lead going into the seventh inning of Game 6. The Cards battled back and tied it in the seventh, but Dodger slugger Mike Marshall made it 5–4 with a towering home run in the bottom of the eighth.

In the ninth, the Cardinals were able to put men on second and third with the red hot Jack Clark (.381 for the series) at the plate. It looked like the perfect time for an intentional walk. Dodger pitcher Tom Niedenfuer (see separate chapter) checked the dugout, asking if he should walk Clark to create a force at any base. Lasorda signalled back, "Pitch to Clark." Niedenfuer proceeded to offer Clark his best stuff. Clark promptly cracked the ball into the stands for a three-run homer to win the game and the pennant.

The Verdict

Even the best managers make mistakes that later haunt them, and Tom Lasorda is no exception. To be sure, he is one of the game's better managers and his record proves this. But in this case, Lasorda took a chance, and on that fateful October day in 1985 he lost.

Gene Mauch, Manager
1964, 1982, and 1986 drives toward World Series

MANAGERIAL RECORD HIGHLIGHTS

YEAR	TEAM	W	L	Pct.	Standing
1964	Phillies	92	70	.568	2
1982	Angels	93	69	.574	1
1986	Angels	92	70	.568	1

Act One

For Gene Mauch's '64 Phillies, it should never have come to this.

There they all were, Jim Bunning and Dick Allen and Cookie Rojas and all the rest, straining to hear the radio broadcast of the final relevant game of the 1964 regular season, a contest between the laughable New York Mets and the St. Louis Cardinals. If the lowly Mets could somehow overtake the Cards, Philadelphia would finish with a share of first place . . . a share they should never have relinquished.

In late September it had all looked great for the Phaithful. The Phils had led by more than six games with only twelve remaining. "PHILS SNIFFING PENNANT PASTRY AS COOKIE REFUSES TO CRUMBLE," went the *Sporting News* headline, referring not only to the optimism around the City of Brotherly Love, but also feisty infielder Rojas' dogged, determined style of play. The franchise had even printed World Series tickets for what was to be the team's first appearance in the fall classic in fourteen years.

But then Mauch had tinkered with the starting rotation. He'd tried pitching his aces Bunning and Chris Short on only two days' rest in the final weeks of the season—and somehow the Phillies had dropped ten in a row. So here they all were. Listening to the radio.

Final score: Cardinals 11, Mets 5. St. Louis had the pennant that had looked for all the world like it belonged to Gene Mauch.

Act Two

For Gene Mauch's '82 Angels, it should never have come to this.

There they all were, Rod Carew and Reggie Jackson and Don Baylor and all the rest, down by a run in the final game of the American League Championship Series against the Brewers, a series from which Milwaukee was supposed to have been all but eliminated. The Angels had taken the first two games of the best-of-five series, and the outcome had seemed clear. One more California victory and Mauch had the first pennant of his 22-year managerial career.

But then an eighth-inning rally in the third game fell short and left Mauch's team on the losing end of a 5–3 score. Angel starter Tommy John got hammered early in the following contest, which went 9–5 Brewers.

Now, in the final game, Mauch had called on reliever Luis Sanchez to protect a slim 3–2 Angel lead. Sanchez had faced a bases-loaded jam in the seventh, but the manager had stuck with his man. And Mauch's man had yielded a two-run single to Cecil Cooper. So here they all were. Down by a run in the ninth in a game many felt should never have been played in the first place.

Final score: Brewers 4, Angels 3. Milwaukee had the pennant that had looked for all the world like it belonged to Gene Mauch.

Act Three

For Gene Mauch's '86 Angels, it should never have come to this.

There they all were, Bob Boone and Reggie Jackson and Wally Joyner and all the rest, down by a run in what was supposed to have been the last game of the American League Championship Series against the Red Sox. A game California had led going into the ninth. A game that would have clinched the pennant for the Angels.

They'd had the champagne ready in the clubhouse. Angel players had been waving towels from the dugout steps, whipping the 64,223 California fans into a frenzy. All had been in readiness for the big celebration. Then starter Mike Witt had yielded a one-out home run to Boston slugger Don Baylor, but recovered by retiring Dwight Evans. Two out. Nobody on. The Angels' lead was intact. Only Boston's Rich Gedman stood between the Angels and a spot in the World Series.

But Mauch had wanted a new pitcher. He dismissed Witt and summoned lefthander Gary Lucas to face Gedman and record the final out. But it didn't work out that way. Lucas' very first pitch struck Gedman. Next, Mauch summoned Donnie Moore to face Boston outfielder Dave Henderson, who had fanned on four pitches his last time up against Witt.

Henderson had no such problems with Moore. He pounced on a low-

and-away forkball (a pitch that sportswriter Dan Shaughnessy reports had starter Witt screaming "from the moment it left [Moore's] hand") and sent it rocketing into the seats in left-center.

To be sure, the Angels had come back with a run of their own in the home half of the inning. But Henderson of all people came back in the eleventh with a sacrifice fly off Moore. That scored the run that put Boston ahead once again.

So here they all were. Down by a run. And the champagne waiting. It seemed like it had been waiting a long time now.

Final score: Red Sox 7, Angels 6. The Sox went on to take the pennant that had looked, for all the world, like it belonged to Gene Mauch.

The Verdict

Gene Mauch is the owner of perhaps the least sought-after managerial record in baseball: He won 1,902 games without ever guiding his team to the World Series. He had his chances, but the sad fact is that his moves, as retold in the three acts of our "drama" above, were not the right ones. Like many of the other goats in this book, Mauch's misadventures seem to have been influenced at least in part by whims of fate. But then again, fate doesn't make you start your two big guns on two days' rest during the most critical weeks of the season.

Mauch belongs on this list.

Joe McCarthy

Joe McCarthy, Manager and
Denny Galehouse, Pitcher

Boston Red Sox
American League Playoff *vs.* Cleveland Indians
October 4, 1948

MANAGERIAL RECORD

YEARS	TEAM	W	L	Pct.
1926–1930	Cubs	442	321	.579
1931–1946	Yankees	1460	867	.627
1948–1950	Red Sox	223	145	.606
	TOTALS	2125	1333	.615

The year is 1948. You're Boston manager Joe McCarthy. Your tough Red Sox outfit has scratched its way back from an 11½-game deficit to tie the Cleveland Indians for first place on the final day of the season. You must select a starting pitcher for the all-important one-game playoff at Fenway Park. Do you:

A. Select from an impressive starting rotation that includes Jack Kramer (18–5), Joe Dobson (16–10), Ellis Kinder (10–7), and Mel Parnell (15–8);

B. Consider asking slugger Ted Williams to take the mound, on the theory that he has the staff's lowest career innings-pitched-to-home run ratio (two innings, zero homers yielded); or

C. Call on anonymous journeyman Denny Galehouse.

McCarthy went for Plan C, and the rest, as they say, is history: Galehouse was bombed, yielding, among other things, a three-run Ken Keltner homer; the Red Sox lost, 8-3, the Indians went on to win the World Series.

How could it happen? In all likelihood, no adequate answer can ever be made. Like Babe Ruth's departure in 1920, Mike Torrez' meatball to light-hitting Yankee shortstop Bucky Dent in 1978, and the Red Sox collapse in the sixth game of the 1986 Series against the Mets, the 1948 playoff game is one of those inscrutable twists of fate Boston fans agonize over for years. The Galehouse affair is not *supposed* to make sense: it happened to the Red Sox.

Fifteen-game-winner Mel Parnell, who would later emerge as one of the league's premier southpaws, vividly recalled McCarthy's move. "I was in bed by nine o'clock the night before and ready to go," he said. "I never dreamed [McCarthy would pick] Galehouse. Neither did Denny. He was dumbfounded. He was shagging flies in the outfield during batting practice when McCarthy sent a clubhouse man for him. When Joe told him, Denny went white as a ghost."

Galehouse was not the only one who found the move hard to believe. Cleveland manager Lou Boudreau later admitted that he suspected McCarthy of playing a trick designed to fool the Indians into preparing for the wrong pitcher. He was sure Boston would produce the "real" starter at the last moment.

McCarthy's postgame attempts to defend his decision to go with Galehouse all looked absurd. The manager claimed, for instance, that since the wind was blowing out to left in Boston that day, he was obliged to go with the right-hander Galehouse. Yet Boston's Jack Kramer threw right-handed, as well—and had won eighteen games for the Sox that year. (It should be noted, too, that Cleveland's Gene Bearden, a lefty, had no problem retiring Boston batters that day.) Then there was the theory that Galehouse was particularly effective against the Indians' lineup. Some opined that this predisposition of McCarthy's had to do with a strong relief appearance against the Tribe Denny had posted about a month before the big game. If that was the rationale, it was a shaky one in a contest of this magnitude. Galehouse was, good outing or no good outing, a mediocre 37-year-old hurler whose main claim to fame was treading water as a member of the pathetic St. Louis Browns, for whom he won 41 games and lost 56.

Whatever reasoning led McCarthy to rely on Galehouse to pitch the most important game of the 1948 season, they probably looked suspect even to the skipper along about the fourth inning. By that time Galehouse had yielded five runs. Boston never led in the game.

The manager was stoic in defeat, but it is fair to say that Galehouse was traumatized by the episode; he would make only two more big-league starts after the 1948 playoff game. McCarthy would endure yet another down-to-the-wire elimination as manager of the Red Sox in 1949, this time at the hands of the New York Yankees.

The Verdict

Two more classic examples of the baseball goat would be hard to find. McCarthy's pitching selection was (and is) baffling; Galehouse, as much victim as perpetrator, was simply the wrong man for the job.

Fred "Bonehead" Merkle

First Base, New York Giants
Regular Season Game *vs.* Chicago Cubs
September 23, 1908

CAREER HIGHLIGHTS

YEAR	TEAM	AVG	G	AB	R	H	2B	3B	HR	RBI
1907	Giants	.255	15	47	0	12	1	0	0	5
1908	Giants	.268	38	41	6	11	2	1	1	7
1909	Giants	.191	79	236	15	45	9	1	0	20
1910	Giants	.292	144	506	75	148	35	14	4	70
1911	Giants	.283	149	541	80	153	24	10	12	84
1912	Giants	.309	129	479	82	148	22	6	11	84
1913	Giants	.261	153	563	78	147	30	12	3	69
1914	Giants	.258	146	512	71	132	25	7	7	63
1915	Giants	.299	140	505	52	151	25	3	4	62
1917	Cubs	.266	146	549	65	146	30	9	3	57
1918	Cubs	.297	129	482	55	143	25	5	3	65
1919	Cubs	.267	133	498	52	133	20	6	3	62
	CAREER TOTALS	.273	1638	5782	720	1580	290	81	61	733

$\mathbf{F}$red Merkle made one baserunning mistake that would torment him for the rest of his playing career—and his life, for that matter. In the heat of the intense National League pennant race of 1908, the New York Giants were playing the first-place Chicago Cubs. The Giants found themselves tied 1–1 in the bottom of the ninth inning with two out, Moose McCormick on third, and Merkle on first. Shortstop Al Bridwell stepped up to the plate and rapped a solid single into center field, scoring McCormick. Merkle stood a few steps off of first, admired his teammate's clutch game-winning hit, and then headed for the dugout.

It looked like the Giants had earned a dramatic victory over their rivals; both teams headed for their respective dugouts. But a few Cub players quickly realized that the game was not over yet—Fred Merkle had neglected to touch second base before leaving the field! How could Bridwell's single stand if there was still a runner legally occupying first base?

The Cubs' Johnny Evers scrounged up a ball and headed for second base to make the force out. However, Giant pitcher Joe McGinnity gave chase and tackled him near the pitcher's mound. McGinnity pried the ball away from Evers and threw it into the crowd. Finally, Evers grabbed another ball and tagged second, at which point umpire Hank O'Day declared Merkle the final out of the ninth inning.

It should be noted that in those days it was customary for umpires to ignore similar technical infractions when they occurred after a game-winning hit. Not this time, though.

The Giants and their fans were furious; the crowd poured onto the field in confusion and rage. The game had to be called, and it went into the record books as a tie. The outraged Giants played the remainder of the season under protest. As fate would have it, the two teams ended the season in a tie for first place. League officials called for a replay of the infamous "Merkle Game" in order to decide the pennant. The Giants lost 4–2, and the New York press lambasted Merkle as the goat who had cost the city the pennant. The papers were merciless to Merkle, and blamed the entire season's outcome on his base-running error. From that day on, teammates, opposing players, and even small children in the street referred to poor Fred as "Bonehead."

Despite the constant jeering and occasional bouts with depression, Merkle played another 16 years in the majors, compiling a respectable lifetime batting average of .273 and playing in five World Series. In fact, in the 1912 World Series, Merkle was involved in another goat-creating game involving Fred Snodgrass (see chapter on Snodgrass).

The Verdict

History is often cruel, but in this case, it was right. Fred Merkle just plain neglected to touch second base when the rules clearly stated that he was supposed to. Merkle lost the game (and, alas, the pennant) for the Giants, and he did it more or less on his own.

Donnie Moore
Pitcher, California Angels
American League Playoffs *vs.* Boston Red Sox
October 12, 1986

YEAR	TEAM	W	L	SV	G	GS	IP	H	HR	BB	SO	ERA
1975	Cubs	0	0	0	4	1	9	12	1	4	8	4.00
1977	Cubs	4	2	0	27	1	49	51	1	18	34	4.04
1978	Cubs	9	7	4	71	1	103	117	7	31	50	4.11
1979	Cubs	1	4	1	39	1	73	95	8	25	43	5.18
1980	Cardinals	1	1	0	11	0	22	25	1	5	10	6.14
1981	Brewers	0	0	0	3	0	4	4	0	4	2	6.75
1982	Braves	3	1	1	16	0	28	32	1	7	17	4.18
1983	Braves	2	3	6	43	0	69	72	6	10	41	3.65
1984	Braves	4	5	16	47	0	64	63	3	18	47	2.95
1985	Angels	8	8	31	65	0	103	91	9	21	72	1.92
1986	Angels	4	5	21	49	0	73	60	10	22	53	2.96
1987	Angels	2	2	5	14	0	27	28	2	13	17	2.67
1988	Angels	5	2	4	27	0	33	48	4	8	22	4.91
CAREER TOTALS		43	40	89	416	4	657	698	53	186	416	3.66

Move over Branca, Terry and Niedenfuer. There's another guy who threw a gopher pitch for a famous home run. California's Donnie Moore gave up the homer that would spark one of the most dramatic comebacks in baseball history.

With a three-games-to-one advantage over Boston in the best-of-seven A.L. playoffs of 1986, the Angels went into Game 5 with heads held high. The franchise, like manager Gene Mauch (see separate chapter), had never won a pennant despite many close moments. It was a long time coming, but it looked like the flag would finally come to Anaheim.

After five and a half innings, the Red Sox were leading Game 5, 2–1. The Angels' hard-nosed veteran Bobby Grich came to bat with one on and hit a shot toward center. Substitute center fielder Dave Henderson sprinted back to the wall and leapt. The ball nestled into his glove but popped out and over the fence when he crashed into the wall. It went for a two-run homer, and a painful one at that. Henderson had made an amazing play to get to the ball. But now, with the score 3–2, Angels, he looked to be just another in a long line of Boston Red Sox goats.

Indeed, the Sox appeared doomed when California added a couple of insurance runs in the bottom of the seventh. But the Sox wouldn't go away. In the top of the ninth, Don Baylor hit a two-run homer to cut the Angels' lead to 5–4. After two outs and a hit batsman, star closer Donnie Moore was summoned from the bullpen to finish the game. He would face the man who made the Angel lead possible, Dave Henderson. Moore worked the count to 2–2. He and the California Angels were now one strike away from taking on the New York Mets in the 82nd World Series. Henderson was swinging feebly while he fouled off a few pitches. Then, unbelievably, he reached out on a forkball and deposited it into the left center stands. His home run put Boston ahead 6–5 and instantly revoked Henderson's goat status.

The Angels tied the game in the bottom of the inning, but the Sox came back to win it in the eleventh on a sacrifice fly by (who else?) Henderson.

Riding the sudden burst of adrenalin, the Red Sox easily won the final two games of the series to capture the A.L. flag. California fans were in a state of shock. Just one more strike from Moore in Game 5 would have won the pennant.

The defeat was the beginning of a tragic fall for Moore. Over the next few years, he lost confidence in his pitching and was released by the Angels. The Royals picked him up but sent him down to the minors. Finally, on June 12, 1989, the Royals released him. Friends said he was devastated by his release and that he was showing signs of a personality disorder. On June 19, he shot and seriously wounded his wife just before turning the gun on himself and committing suicide.

The Verdict

Like Dennis Eckersley in 1988, Moore was his team's ace stopper and was brought into a crucial game for only one purpose: to send the Red Sox back home for the winter. He didn't. Tragic as his story turned out to be, Donnie Moore earned his spot on this list.

Bob Moose

Pitcher

Pittsburgh Pirates

National League Playoffs *vs*. Cincinnati Reds

October 11, 1972

YEAR	TEAM	W	L	G	GS	IP	H	HR	BB	SO	ERA
1967	Pirates	1	0	2	2	15	14	1	4	7	3.60
1968	Pirates	8	12	38	22	171	136	5	41	126	2.74
1969	Pirates	14	3	44	19	170	149	9	62	165	2.91
1970	Pirates	11	10	28	27	190	186	14	64	119	3.98
1971	Pirates	11	7	30	18	140	169	12	35	68	4.11
1972	Pirates	13	10	31	30	226	213	11	47	144	2.91
1973	Pirates	12	13	33	29	201	219	11	70	111	3.54
1974	Pirates	1	5	7	6	36	59	4	7	15	7.50
1975	Pirates	2	2	23	5	68	63	4	25	34	3.71
1976	Pirates	3	9	53	2	88	100	4	32	38	3.68
	CAREER TOTALS	76	71	289	160	1305	1308	75	387	827	3.50

1972 saw the Pittsburgh Pirates and Cincinnati Reds each run away with their respective divisions in the National League. Pittsburgh, which finished 11 games ahead of the second-place Chicago Cubs, was heavily favored to win the National League Championship Series.

The Pirates defeated Cincy easily in the first game, 5–1, but floundered in Game 2 when starter Bob Moose couldn't get a single out in the first inning. His five hits and four runs allowed gave the Reds the winning margin; the final score was 5–3. For the unfortunate Moose, all this was but a taste of bad things to come.

The Pirates squeaked by Cincinnati, 3–2 in Game 3, but dropped the next game as Ross Grimsley pitched a complete-game two-hitter to win 7–1. This tied the series at two games apiece and forced a fifth and final game in Cincinnati.

The Pirates jumped on the board in the second inning of the decisive game for a 2–0 lead, then added another in the fourth. But the Reds chipped away at the lead, and going into the bottom of the ninth it was 3–2, Pittsburgh.

Pirate pitchers Steve Blass and Ramon Hernandez had done well, but manager Bill Virdon wasn't taking any chances. He motioned for Dave Giusti, proud possessor of a 1.92 ERA during the regular season, to finish off the Big Red Machine. But he couldn't. Johnny Bench rocked Giusti's fourth pitch for an opposite-field home run to tie the game at 3. The Cincinnati fans went crazy. Giusti lost his composure and allowed two straight singles. That put the winning run in scoring position with nobody out. Virdon had seen enough; he brought in Moose, the man who had allowed four runs without recording an out in Game 2.

Moose almost got out of the inning. He got two quick fly outs, with pinch-runner George Foster tagging up and taking third on one of them. Pinch-hitter Hal McRae then strode to the plate with men on first and third and two outs. The count stood at 1–1 when Moose threw wild, bouncing a pitch over the head of catcher Manny Sanguillen. Foster scored from third easily and the Reds had the pennant.

In the glum Pirates' clubhouse after the game, Moose said of his wild pitch, "I was trying to waste the pitch by throwing a slider outside. When I let it go, I knew it was outside where I wanted it. I didn't think it was that low, but when it started going down I figured it would bounce up and hit Manny in the stomach. But it took a crazy hop over his head. How many times have you seen a bounce that high?"

The underdog Reds had snatched the N.L. flag away from the Pirates; they went on to extend the World Series against the Oakland A's to seven games. Pirate fans never got over the queasy feeling that the Series slot should have been theirs.

Moose's horrendous playoff performance was the low point in a career marked by extreme ups and downs. In 1969 he threw a no-hitter against the Miracle Mets, yet he ended the '72 playoff series with an obscene ERA of 54.00.

The Verdict

Dave Giusti should probably share the 1972 National League playoff goat distinction with Bob Moose for serving up Johnny Bench's home run and yielding two singles. But as with Bill Buckner's situation in 1986, people tend to forget that the score was tied before the game-ending play, and that more than one person helped blow the lead.

Marv Throneberry

New York Mets
The 1962 Season

Ｈow bad can a team get?

There have been some lousy baseball teams in the twentieth century, but it's safe to say that none has approached the legendary levels of awful play achieved by the 1962 New York Mets. Some full-roster teams appearing in this book were named goats because of a collapse down the stretch in ·a pennant race; sportswriters responding to our poll named the Mets to the list because they collapsed on *Opening Day*, and continued to do so at a record pace for the balance of the season.

You want numbers? How about a team winning percentage of .250—lower by eleven points than the entire National League *batting* average that year? How about a pitching staff whose "ace," Roger Craig, won ten games and lost twenty-four? (Craig had another twenty-game loser, Al Jackson, to back him up in the rotation.) How about finishing sixty and one-half games behind the pennant-winning San Francisco Giants?

To fully understand the strange doings in and around the Polo Grounds during the 1962 season, one has to have a little background information. New York had been bereft of a National League franchise since the departure of the Giants and Dodgers for California after the 1957 season. The sense of betrayal felt by many New Yorkers by these moves is hard to imagine now; for decades, residents of the city had taken on team allegiances with a fanaticism that approached religious intensity. You were either a Yankee fan, a Dodger fan, or a Giant fan. When two of those three teams abandoned the city, a lot of people lost not only a morning box score, but parts of themselves, as well.

So it was that the New York Mets—bearing Yankee pinstripes, Dodger blue, and Giant orange—were greeted with joy and perhaps a little more optimism than they warranted in the spring of 1962. They posted a passable 12–15 record during spring training, leading some of the more gullible New York faithful to believe they might be capable of competing at the major league level.

The Mets set a record that year for fewest victories in a 162-game season (40). Their longest winning streak of the year was three. They lost games because of terrible pitching (the staff yielded ten runs or more twenty-three times), terrible hitting (the team average was easily the lowest in the league), and terrible fielding (Met glovemen posted an abysmal .967 team mark). "We found a different way to lose every day," confessed pitcher Ken McKenzie. Manager Casey Stengel's famous question was perhaps more telling: "Can't anybody here play this game?" And yet . . .

And yet they drew nearly a million fans. Strange fans, perhaps, fans who came not expecting to cheer a victory but prepared to mount a sustained torrent of abuse in the face of inevitable defeat. But fans nonetheless. Despite the numbing regularity of their defeats, despite fielding a ragtag collections of has-beens (Gil Hodges, Richie Ashburn, Gene Woodling), hasn't-beens (Marvelous Marv Throneberry, Hobie Landrith) and assorted unidentifiables (Cliff Cook, Choo-Choo Coleman), and despite a laughably disorganized front office—a front office that somehow managed, for instance, to obtain catcher Harry Chiti from Cleveland for a player to be named later who turned out to be Chiti himself—despite all this, the Mets were loved. It was an unusual relationship the Mets shared with their many fans, a relationship that would prompt first baseman Throneberry to reflect on his anti-hero role at season's end. "People came to the park to holler at me, just like Mantle and Maris," he said. "I drew people to games. (But) I took a lot of abuse."

It all said something about baseball. And about New York.

The Verdict

Guilty as charged.

Tom Niedenfuer

Pitcher, Los Angeles Dodgers
National League Playoffs *vs.* St. Louis Cardinals
October 16, 1985

YEAR	TEAM	W	L	G	IP	H	HR	BB	SO	SV	ERA
1981	Dodgers	3	1	17	26	25	1	6	12	2	3.81
1982	Dodgers	3	4	55	70	71	3	25	60	9	2.70
1983	Dodgers	8	3	66	95	55	6	29	66	11	1.89
1984	Dodgers	2	5	33	47	39	3	23	45	11	2.49
1985	Dodgers	7	9	64	106	86	6	24	102	19	2.72
1986	Dodgers	6	6	60	80	86	11	29	55	11	3.71
1987	Dodgers	1	0	15	16	13	1	9	10	1	2.81
1987	Orioles	3	5	45	52	55	11	22	37	13	5.02
1988	Orioles	3	4	52	59	59	8	19	40	18	3.51
1989	Mariners	0	3	25	36	36	7	15	15	0	6.75
	CAREER TOTALS	36	40	432	587	587	57	201	442	95	3.28

Most of the pros in this book found themselves in the position of blowing it bigtime in the national spotlight just once in a career. No doubt once was enough! It's bad enough to have one BGE (Baseball Goat Experience) in a key situation. But when a player finds himself wearing two sets of horns in a matter of three days—and in the National League Championship Series, no less—that's enough to make one wonder about the good intentions of the baseball gods.

Los Angeles Dodgers reliever Tom Niedenfuer must have wondered. When 1985 came to a close, all that was clear was that the St. Louis Cardinals had won the pennant . . . and that Niedenfuer had fallen victim to some of the toughest championship-game twists of fate in history.

Here's what happened. L.A. had won the first two games of the series behind strong performances from Fernando Valenzuela and Orel Hershiser. The Cardinals came back strong in the next two games, however, winning 4–2 and 12–2, respectively. That set the stage for the fifth game, which was to be held in St. Louis.

The Cards got to Valenzuela early this time, and led 2–0 until the fourth, when the Dodgers came up with a two-run rally of their own. That's how it stayed until the ninth inning, when Dodger skipper Tommy Lasorda signaled for Niedenfuer. The righthander had posted a career-high 19 saves for L.A. that year, and was usually quite dependable in shutting the opposition down when the game was on the line. Not this time, though. Cardinal shortstop Ozzie Smith, not noted for his longball capacity, hit the first lefthanded home run of his career. The Cardinals led the series three games to two.

That would have been bad enough, but there was still the matter of the sixth game. In that contest, L.A. took a slim 5–4 lead into the ninth and was bidding to extend the series to a seventh and deciding game in Dodger Stadium. But Niedenfuer, who had relieved Hershiser in the seventh, got into trouble. He had two out, but he also had two men on. And he had St. Louis slugger Jack Clark at the plate. Manager Lasorda made the decision to have Niedenfuer pitch to Clark. The result was a towering home run that may have landed in a different time zone.

That homer provided the winning margin. The Dodgers' season was over, and Tom Niedenfuer had accounted for two of L.A.'s four defeats by yielding two consecutive ninth-inning St. Louis home runs.

The double-whammy was a crushing blow to the Dodgers, who had seemed to be in control of the series. For Niedenfuer, the pitch selection may have been the problem. "I was thinking I'd fool him by throwing a fastball," he said afterwards, and then, admitting that the trickery hadn't quite panned out, acknowledged the awesome scale of the Clark blast. "The only way that ball would have stayed in the ballpark," said the pitcher, "is if it hit the blimp."

The Verdict

First things first: the real event here is not Smith's
home run, for which Niedenfuer could have achieved
a measure of atonement in the subsequent game, but
Clark's blast. It is fair to say that Niedenfuer grooved
the fastball to the dangerous slugger, and so deserves
a place here. It is also fair to say, however, that with
two outs and first base open, many managers would
never have given Clark the chance to hit.

Rickey Henderson

Oakland Athletics
World Series *vs*. Cincinnati Reds
October 16–20, 1990

In 1988, manager Tony LaRussa and his Oakland A's swept the Boston Red Sox in the playoffs only to be embarrassed by the underdog Los Angeles Dodgers in the World Series. Just two years later, history repeated itself. The A's swept the Sox again, only to fall once more in the 1990 October Classic, victims of a sweep at the hands of the scrappy and very underrated Cincinnati Reds. Maybe the A's should think twice about going all-out against the Sox.

When a team as highly favored as the A's is the victim of a sweep in a high-pressure series, the first word that comes to mind is "choke." This might have been the public's perception of the A's performance in the 1990 World Series, but it wasn't necessarily the case. The Reds had a lot going for them.

Cincinnati started off with a bang, roughing up A's ace Dave Stewart and winning Game 1 at Riverfront Stadium, 7–0. The confident A's weren't fazed at all. They just needed to get used to the speedy, heads-up style of the National League champs. No problem.

The next game was a squeaker, but the Reds pulled it off once again. This time the score was 5–4; Cincy catcher Joe Oliver delivered a clutch RBI single in the bottom of the tenth to put the Reds up two games to none. The A's shrugged the loss off.

The Series moved to Oakland for Game 3. The Reds hammered Oakland pitching for fourteen hits while routing them, 8–3, in their own park. The A's began to wonder if there might really be cause for concern. Suddenly, the team who just a few days earlier had been given very little chance to pull off even one victory against Oakland's mighty lineup, was one game away from winning their first world championship in fourteen years.

Game 4 began with Stewart back on the mound for Oakland. The big righthander was not about to let his team be humiliated by a four-game sweep. He bore down, pitching scoreless ball for seven innings before giving up two runs (only one earned). But Cincy pitching—excellent in the first three games—was outstanding in Game 4. Jose Rijo allowed only two hits in 8⅓ innings, struck out nine, and gave up just one run. Stopper Randy Myers took the mound in the ninth and nailed it down for the Reds. The final score: 2–1. The sweep was complete, and the A's were sent home scratching their heads.

The Verdict

Folks tend to forget just how good a team the 1990 Cincinnati Reds really were. During the course of the season, Oakland's big bats (Canseco, McGwire, Henderson) and big guns (Stewart, Eckersley, Welch) dominated the headlines, while the Reds quietly led the National League West for 162 straight games with consistant overall play. The Reds played as a team, while Oakland played as a group of individual stars.

Mickey Owen
Catcher, Brooklyn Dodgers
World Series *vs.* New York Yankees
October 5, 1941

YEAR	TEAM	AVG	G	AB	R	H	2B	3B	HR	RBI
1937	Cardinals	.231	80	234	17	54	4	2	0	20
1938	Cardinals	.267	122	397	45	106	25	2	4	36
1939	Cardinals	.259	131	344	32	89	18	2	3	35
1940	Cardinals	.264	117	307	27	81	16	2	0	27
1941	Dodgers	.231	128	386	32	89	15	2	1	44
1942	Dodgers	.259	133	421	53	109	16	3	0	44
1943	Dodgers	.260	106	365	31	95	11	2	0	54
1944	Dodgers	.273	130	461	43	126	20	3	1	42
1945	Dodgers	.286	24	84	5	24	9	0	0	11
1949	Cubs	.273	62	198	15	54	9	3	2	18
1950	Cubs	.243	86	259	22	63	11	0	2	21
1951	Cubs	.184	58	125	10	23	6	0	0	15
1954	Red Sox	.235	32	68	6	16	3	0	1	11
	CAREER TOTALS	.255	1209	3649	338	929	163	21	14	378

The New York Yankees were ahead two games to one in the 1941 World Series, but the Brooklyn Dodgers were poised to tie it up, leading Game 4 by a score of 4–3 in the top of the ninth. Brooklyn's big righthander Hugh Casey had sparkled, coming on in relief of Johnny Allen in the fifth and holding the Yanks at bay for four innings. He retired the first two Yankee batters in the ninth. The third Yankee batter, Tommy Henrich, was the only hurdle left for Casey and the Dodgers. One out would end the game and tie up the Series.

Casey got Henrich in the hole right away, 1–2. His next pitch was a big, sweeping screwball that hit the ground about a foot in front of the plate. Henrich was completely fooled and swung wildly for strike three.

Unfortunately for Brooklyn, Dodger catcher Mickey Owen was apparently also completely fooled. Brooklyn fans watched in horror as Henrich scampered over to first on Owen's dropped third strike. It was all downhill from there for the Dodgers, as Joe DiMaggio stepped up and cracked a solid single. Next came Charlie Keller, who doubled in two runs to give the Yanks the 5–4 lead. Bill Dickey walked and Joe Gordon doubled in another two runs to make it 7–4, Yankees before the final (and fourth) out of the inning was recorded.

The Dodgers had one more chance in the bottom of the ninth, but the momentum had swung the way of the Yankees. Brooklyn did not score and the Yankees took a 3 games to 1 Series lead. The next day, "Tiny" Bonham and the Yanks finished off the Dodgers by holding them to just four hits. The Yankees had won their fifth World Series in six years.

Meanwhile, Mickey Owen's fan mail turned to hate mail. Dodger fans had waited for more than 40 years for a World Series title, and Owen was an easy target for their rage. Dodger fans would have to wait another fourteen years for a championship.

Some say that Casey and Owen got their signs mixed up, with Owen expecting a curve instead of a screwball. Another theory is that Casey threw a spitter. In any event, Hugh Casey's pitch was not exactly down the middle. Years later, Owen said "I played pro ball for more than 20 years and considered myself a pretty fair country catcher. My record proves it. That third strike from Hugh Casey was really a dandy, and if the ball had carried 24 inches or so further, I would have caught it easily."

The Verdict

Casey's pitch was very wild, and it's hard to believe Tommy Henrich swung at it in the first place. If it was a spitter, then hang the goat horns on Hugh Casey. If it was a case of crossed up signs, hang 'em on Casey and Owen.

Roger Peckinpaugh
Shortstop, Washington Senators
World Series *vs.* Pittsburgh Pirates
October 7–15, 1925

CAREER HIGHLIGHTS

YEAR	TEAM	AVG	G	AB	R	H	2B	3B	HR	RBI
1912	Indians	.212	69	236	18	50	4	1	1	22
1913	Yankees	.268	95	340	35	91	10	7	1	32
1914	Yankees	.223	157	570	55	127	14	6	3	51
1915	Yankees	.220	142	540	67	119	18	7	5	44
1916	Yankees	.255	145	552	65	141	22	8	4	58
1917	Yankees	.260	148	543	63	141	24	7	0	41
1918	Yankees	.231	122	446	59	103	15	3	0	43
1919	Yankees	.305	122	453	89	138	20	2	7	33
1920	Yankees	.270	139	534	109	144	26	6	8	54
1921	Yankees	.288	149	577	128	166	25	7	8	71
1922	Senators	.254	147	520	62	132	14	4	2	48
1923	Senators	.264	154	568	73	150	18	4	2	62
1924	Senators	.272	155	523	72	142	20	5	2	73
1925	Senators	.294	126	422	67	124	16	4	4	64
1926	Senators	.238	57	147	19	35	4	1	1	14
	CAREER TOTALS	.259	2011	7233	1006	1876	256	75	48	739

As captain of the Washington Senators in 1925, Roger Peckinpaugh was named the American League Most Valuable Player, leading his team to its second pennant in as many years. Throughout the regular season, the scrappy shortstop batted .294 and did a superb fielding job, finishing among the league leaders in assists and committing only a handful of errors. However, the baseball gods must have decided that Roger looked a little *too* smooth that year. In the 1925 Series, he set a record that still stands: a total of eight errors in a World Series.

The Senators, who for years resided in or around the American League basement, had recently put together a team of contenders that copped the world championship from the favored New York Giants in 1924. Their roster included the aging but still formidable fireballer Walter Johnson, centerfielder Sam Rice, leftfielder Goose Goslin, and 28-year-old second baseman/manager Bucky "Boy Manager" Harris. With Harris' youthful enthusiasm and Peckinpaugh's 15 years of big-league experience, the two established themselves as wise and gutsy leaders of the surprisingly successful Washington squad.

On October 7, 1925, Peckinpaugh and the Senators faced a tough Pittsburgh Pirates outfit in Game 1 of the World Series. Behind future Hall of Famer Johnson, the Senators won this game easily by a 4–1 score. Pittsburgh evened it up by rallying in the eighth inning of Game 2 to win 3–2. Then the Senators pulled ahead, winning the next two games in a row with Johnson throwing a masterful shutout in Game 4. But the resourceful Pirates surprised the Senators by handily pulling off two quick wins (of 6–3 and 3–2) to even the Series at three victories apiece. The final, deciding game would be played at Pittsburgh's Forbes Field on October 15; Johnson would make his third start of the series, taking on Vic Aldridge. *The New York Times* would declare that contest both "the best and the worst game of baseball ever played in this country."

It was a miserable, rainy day. Fog shrouded the muddy field. Today's groundskeepers would have shuddered at the thought of leveling the Forbes Field infield that day. But a 40,000-plus sellout crowd braved the abysmal weather to witness the showdown. The game would go on.

Both teams scratched out some weather-assisted offense; going into the bottom of the seventh, the Senators were ahead 6–4. Eddie Moore stepped up for the Pirates and hit a routine pop-up to Peckinpaugh's territory, but Roger muffed the simple play and Moore wound up on second with no outs. It was the unprecedented seventh error of the Series for Peckinpaugh—and it would not be his last.

Moore scored on Max Carey's double, and Carey then scored on Pie Traynor's triple. By the end of the seventh, the score was tied up 6–6.

In the top of the eighth, Peckinpaugh made a bid to atone for his poor fielding when he homered to left. But with two outs in the bottom of the inning, the Pirates tied it up again on a pair of doubles.

Then disaster struck. Johnson walked Moore. With Washington still needing only one out to get out of the eighth inning, Max Carey rapped a hard grounder to Peckinpaugh that should have been that inning-ending out. But Roger threw it over Bucky Harris' head to load the bases. Kiki Cuyler then ripped a double down the line to make the score 9–7, Pirates.

Washington failed to score in the ninth. The Pirates were world champs, and league MVP Roger Peckinpaugh was the goat of the World Series.

Goose Goslin later recalled, "Eight errors. He was jinxed. Before the Series started, he was named the Most Valuable Player in the American League. He was a great shortstop. Made miraculous plays for us all season, hit about .300, and then they put the old hex on him by giving him that award before the Series instead of after it."

The Verdict

Being a normally slick fielder makes it ironic, and the fact that '25 was a career year adds to the irony, but Peckinpaugh truly deserves to wear the horns for his performance in the World Series that year. Not only did his two errors prove disastrous in Game 7, but his six additional ones contributed to at least two other Washington losses.

Johnny Pesky
Shortstop
Boston Red Sox
World Series *vs.* St. Louis Cardinals
October 15, 1946

YEAR	TEAM	AVG	G	AB	R	H	2B	3B	HR	RBI
1942	Red Sox	.331	147	620	105	205	29	9	2	51
1946	Red Sox	.335	153	621	115	208	43	4	2	55
1947	Red Sox	.324	155	638	106	207	27	8	0	39
1948	Red Sox	.281	143	565	124	159	26	6	3	55
1949	Red Sox	.306	148	604	111	185	27	7	2	69
1950	Red Sox	.312	127	490	112	153	22	6	1	49
1951	Red Sox	.313	131	480	93	150	20	6	3	41
1952	Red Sox	.149	25	67	10	10	2	0	0	2
1952	Tigers	.254	69	177	26	45	4	0	1	9
1953	Tigers	.292	103	308	43	90	22	1	2	24
1954	Tigers	.176	20	17	5	3	0	0	1	1
1954	Senators	.253	49	158	17	40	4	3	0	9
	CAREER TOTALS	.307	1270	4745	867	1455	226	50	17	404

Only one of a long string of Boston Red Sox players who earned goat status, shortstop Johnny Pesky has the dubious distinction of being one of the team's first. Throughout the first two decades of the twentieth century, the Sox had dominated the major leagues, at one point winning the World Series four times in eight years. When owner Harry Frazee (see separate chapter) sold Babe Ruth in 1920 to the New York Yankees for $100,000 in order to finance his musical *No No, Nanette*, the Boston Red Sox began a new era of astounding mediocrity.

But Ted Williams came to town in 1939 and with him came a new enthusiasm. The team began to contend again, and Red Sox fans soon grew hungry for a championship.

1946 looked to be the year. The Sox won 104 games and ran away with the American League pennant. Pesky was coming off a torrid year in which he led the American League with 205 hits and placed third with a .335 batting average. Not bad for just his second season in the majors.

With the likes of Dom DiMaggio, Bobby Doerr, Williams and Pesky, the Sox were favored to beat the St. Louis Cardinals in the World Series. But the scrappy Cardinals proved much tougher than originally anticipated, winning Games 2, 4, and 6, necessitating a final, deciding Game 7 on October 15th in St. Louis.

This final game was neck-and-neck as both teams scraped away at each other, winding up with a 3–3 tie going into the bottom of the eighth. The Cards put a runner on first as Enos Slaughter singled to start the inning, but seemed to have fumbled their golden opportunity when the next two batters were retired.

Harry "The Hat" Walker came to the plate and smashed a sinking line drive into left center field that was picked up by substitute centerfielder Leon Culberson. Slaughter had been running with the pitch and was already halfway between third and home by the time Johnny Pesky got the weak relay throw from Culberson. Hesitating just slightly, Pesky threw home to no avail. Slaughter had scored and the Cards had a one-run lead. In the top of the ninth, the Red Sox put two men on with one out, but were finally shut down. The Cardinals had beaten the odds to take the world championship.

After the game Williams wept and waved off reporters, Doerr sulked, and DiMaggio just sat and looked at the floor. Pesky then announced "I'm the goat. It's my fault. I had the ball in my hand. I hesitated and gave Slaughter six steps..."

His teammates knew it wasn't Pesky's fault—Slaughter had an incredible jump on the pitch and Culberson, a utility player, barely lobbed the ball to Pesky. It should also be pointed out that Pesky's slight hesitation has grown to legendary status in the 46 years since, as multiple generations have passed the story along. It is now common to hear about "Pesky's double-clutch." But footage of the play suggests that Slaughter would have beaten the throw in any case. Still, when Pesky's locker room quote appeared in the papers the next day, the public latched onto him as the goat of the 1946 World Series.

The Verdict

Johnny Pesky's worst mistake that day had nothing to do with slightly delaying his throw home. His biggest error was declaring himself "the goat" in a room full of headline-hungry reporters. It made a good headline, but it didn't tell the real story.

Dick Allen

Philadelphia Phillies
1964 Pennant Drive

THE LOSING STREAK, DAY BY DAY:

Date	Winner	Losing Pitcher
September 21	Reds 1–0	Mahaffey
September 22	Reds 9–2	Short
September 23	Reds 6–4	Bennett
September 24	Braves 5–3	Bunning
September 25	Braves 7–5	Short
September 26	Braves 6–4	Mahaffey
September 27	Braves 14–8	Bunning
September 28	Cardinals 5–1	Short
September 29	Cardinals 4–2	Bennett
September 30	Cardinals 8–5	Bunning

How much did it hurt to be a baseball fan in Philadelphia in 1964? With only fifteen games left to play, the Phillies blew a six-and-a-half-game lead by losing ten straight games, allowing the St. Louis Cardinals to take the pennant all of baseball had been sure would go to the Phils.

It had been an autumn of great—perhaps excessive—pride in Philadelphia. The first-place team was so confident that World Series tickets had already been printed by early September. Bulldozers were already stationed in the park, ready to make room for extra field boxes. Players had bought hunting rifles as Series presents to themselves. Considering the events that followed, one must assume the off-season hunting treks were pretty half-hearted.

In late September, a six-and-a-half-game lead still intact, the Phillies began their last homestand of the season against the Reds and the Braves. The first game with the Reds on September 21 was lost when Chico Ruiz stole home for the only run of the game. It was a freak play, almost accidental, and it was accompanied by crossed-up signs and general pandemonium from both teams. But it worked. Ruiz slid home safely and the Phillies began an epic downward slide of their own.

By the end of the homestand, the Phillies had lost three to the Reds and four to the Braves; their own fans were booing them now, and they actually looked forward to finishing the season on the road. Though the location of the games changed, the Phillies continued down the same losing path, dropping three more to the Cardinals. That made ten losses in ten days. At least, optimists reasoned, they were consistent.

What was the cause of these ten days in baseball hell? Much has been made of manager Gene Mauch's overuse of his two ace hurlers, Jim Bun-

141

ning and Chris Short, to the point of exhaustion (see chapter on Mauch). Trying to squeeze out just one win, Mauch used both men with only two days rest during that late September stretch, but neither pitcher could win a single game.

To make matters worse, the defense wasn't holding up behind the pitchers. Fielding errors and poor base running abounded. It seemed as if everyone wanted a hand in the losses, even Most Valuable Player candidate Johnny Callison, who let a winning run score when a fly ball bounced off his glove.

After they finished their final game, the Phillies had one last shred of hope. If the 53–108 New York Mets could beat the 92–69 St. Louis Cardinals—an unlikely event—there would be a three-way tie for first place: the Phillies, the Reds, and the Cardinals, necessitating a round-robin playoff to determine the pennant. As it turned out, the Cards trounced the Mets, 11–5, taking the pennant and sending Gene Mauch and the Phillies home for a long winter of second-guessing. Philadelphians would forever refer to 1964 as the year of the Great Phillie Phlop.

The Verdict

Guilty as charged.

Babe Ruth
Outfield, New York Yankees
World Series *vs.* St. Louis Cardinals
October 10, 1926

CAREER HIGHLIGHTS

YEAR	TEAM	AVG	G	AB	R	H	2B	3B	HR	RBI
1919	Red Sox	.322	130	432	103	139	34	12	29	114
1920	Yankees	.376	142	458	158	172	36	9	54	137
1921	Yankees	.378	152	540	177	204	44	16	59	171
1923	Yankees	.393	152	522	151	205	45	13	41	130
1924	Yankees	.378	153	529	143	200	39	7	46	121
1926	Yankees	.372	152	495	139	184	30	5	47	146
1927	Yankees	.356	151	540	158	192	29	8	60	164
1930	Yankees	.359	145	518	150	186	28	9	49	153
1931	Yankees	.373	145	534	149	199	31	3	46	163
1932	Yankees	.341	133	457	120	156	13	5	41	137
	CAREER TOTALS	.342	2503	8399	2174	2873	506	136	714	2209

The immortal Babe Ruth . . . a goat? It can't be true!

But it is so. Ruth squandered a golden opportunity for his team to win the 1926 World Series when he inexplicably tried to steal second base with two out in the bottom of the ninth of the deciding game.

The St. Louis Cardinals were in a three game tie with the New York Yankees in the best-of-seven series. In the seventh and deciding game, the pre-Gashouse Gang Cards held a 3–2 lead going into the bottom of the seventh inning. But the Yanks threatened when they loaded the bases with two outs. 39-year-old future Hall of Famer Grover Cleveland "Old Pete" Alexander was summoned from the bullpen to deal with Yankee Tony Lazzeri. Apparently hung over from the Cardinal victory celebration of the night before, Old Pete looked to observers like death warmed over on the mound. But the war horse struck out Lazzeri on four pitches to end the threat.

Alexander breezed in the eighth and got two quick outs in the ninth to bring the Cards to the brink of victory. Babe Ruth came to bat with his team down by one run. Alexander pitched around him and gave up a two-out walk—Ruth's eleventh of the series. Up stepped Yankee Bob Meusel, a dangerous clutch hitter who batted a solid .315 during the regular season. He represented the game-winning—and championship-winning—run.

The robust Mr. Ruth, not exactly a speed demon, had stolen just eleven bases during the regular season. Earlier in the Series, however, he had succeeded in executing the only Yankee stolen base. Maybe his confidence was up, maybe he had done one too many bourbon shots in the dugout—whatever the reason, the Bambino took it upon himself to break for second as Alexander delivered the first pitch to Meusel. He had received no signal from the Yankee dugout. Catcher Bob O'Farrell easily gunned down Ruth for the third out. The Series was history.

Rogers Hornsby, the Cardinals' second baseman-manager who made that final putout, later said, "I'll always remember putting the ball on him. He didn't say a word. He didn't even look around or up at me. He just picked himself off the ground and walked away."

The Verdict

In the aftermath of the World Series, Ruth could offer no explanation for his bullet-headed play. Yankee PR man Ed Barrow deemed it the only dumb play of Ruth's career, which may be true considering the countless games that Ruth won for the Yankees over the years. For his performance in at least one game—a crucial one—the Bambino wore the goat horns.

Bob Stanley

Calvin Schiraldi & Bob Stanley

Pitchers
Boston Red Sox
World Series *vs.* New York Mets
October 25, 1986

1986 WORLD SERIES, GAME 6 LINE SCORE:

INNING	1	2	3	4	5	6	7	8	9	10	R	H	E
Boston	1	1	0	0	0	0	1	0	0	2	5	13	3
New York	0	0	0	0	2	0	0	1	0	3	6	8	2

The Boston Red Sox were just a few innings away from winning their first world championship in 68 years. It was the seventh inning of the sixth game of the 1986 World Series, the Sox were leading, and all was well ... until starter Roger Clemens got a blister on his finger; he could no longer throw his slider. Boston manager John McNamara decided to yank Roger.

Young Calvin Schiraldi, who had been virtually unhittable in the second half of the season, relieved Clemens. Pitching in the eighth, he loaded up the bases on a single, an error, and an intentional walk to Keith Hernandez. Gary Carter delivered a long sacrifice fly to tie the game up.

And it stayed tied until the top of the tenth. Dave Henderson, Boston's playoff hero (see chapter on Donnie Moore), led off with a monster home run to left. (People are still trying to figure out how to bottle and sell what got into Dave Henderson during the 1986 postseason.) Wade Boggs then doubled and Marty Barrett singled him in to add an insurance run. Going into the bottom of the tenth holding a 5–3 lead, all the Sox needed were three outs.

Schiraldi got Wally Backman to line out to left. Then Keith Hernandez flied to center. Suddenly, the Red Sox were just three strikes away from their first world championship since 1918.

The champagne was being readied in the Boston clubhouse for the post-game celebration. Meanwhile, New York outfielder Kevin Mitchell was out of uniform, eating a hot dog, and on the phone, making reservations to leave town. Hernandez was drinking a beer and smoking a butt in solitude.

With two outs and nobody on, Schiraldi had Gary Carter 0–2—the proverbial one strike away—when Carter hit a broken bat single to left field. It looked as though a Met rally was in the works, and Mitchell was summoned to pinch hit. He threw down the phone and quickly got dressed, smearing mustard on his uniform. The Mets' big utility man came through and delivered a solid single. Then MVP-to-be Ray Knight got a single after having an 0–2 count on him. This scored Carter and sent Mitchell to third. With his team's lead now cut to one run, John McNamara had seen enough of Schiraldi and motioned to the bullpen.

Bob "Steamer" Stanley came in to pitch to Mookie Wilson with Knight at first and Mitchell on third. To the horror of Boston fans, Stanley and catcher Rich Gedman got their signs crossed up and Stanley's pitch went to the backstop. Mitchell scored the tying run and Knight went to second base.

While Mets fans jumped for joy, Red Sox fans groaned. The champagne was hastily hauled out of the clubhouse. The momentum had swung. It seemed that by hook or by crook, the Mets would find a way to win this game.

With the score now tied, Stanley delivered to Wilson. After what seemed like hundreds of foul balls, Mookie hit his famous roller towards baseball's future all-time goat, Bill Buckner at first base (see separate chapter). The ball snuck under poor Bill's mitt, the winning run scored, and the World Series was sent to a seventh, deciding game. With the wind knocked out of them from the gut-wrenching Game 6, the Red Sox bowed to the Mets in the final game, 8–5.

The Verdict

Bill Buckner missing Wilson's grounder? Big
deal. The hapless Red Sox conceded Game 6 a
few plays earlier, when Schiraldi and Stanley
buckled under pressure. Schiraldi, a youngster, at
least had the excuse of inexperience; several
teammates observed that he simply wasn't the
same overpowering pitcher once he entered
postseason play. But Stanley, a respected veteran,
should have been able to close the door.
He couldn't.

Fred Snodgrass
Outfield
New York Giants
World Series *vs.* Boston Red Sox
October 16, 1912

YEAR	TEAM	AVG	G	AB	R	H	2B	3B	HR	RBI
1908	Giants	.250	6	4	2	1	0	0	0	1
1909	Giants	.300	28	70	10	21	5	0	1	6
1910	Giants	.321	123	396	69	127	22	8	2	44
1911	Giants	.294	151	534	83	157	27	10	1	77
1912	Giants	.269	146	535	91	144	24	9	3	69
1913	Giants	.291	141	457	65	133	21	6	3	49
1914	Giants	.263	113	392	54	103	20	4	0	44
1915	Giants	.194	80	252	36	49	9	0	0	20
1915	Braves	.278	23	79	10	22	2	0	0	9
1916	Braves	.249	112	382	33	95	13	5	1	32
	CAREER TOTALS	.275	923	3101	453	852	143	42	11	351

In Lawrence Ritter's excellent book, *The Glory of Their Times*, Fred Snodgrass reflects on what it was like to be remembered as a goat:

"For over half a century I've had to live with the fact that I dropped a ball in a World Series—'Oh yes, you're the guy that dropped that fly ball, aren't you?'—and for years and years, whenever I'd be introduced to somebody, they'd start to say something and then stop, you know, afraid to hurt my feelings. But nevertheless, those were wonderful years . . . ."

Like most of the people profiled in this book, Snodgrass had reason to doubt the benign intentions of Fate. He wasn't lucky enough to be a Don Larsen, or a Bill Mazeroski, or a Kirk Gibson. At the age of 25, his young career looking up, he dropped a crucial fly ball in the World Series.

It was the eighth and deciding game of the 1912 World Series. The Giants and Red Sox had clawed at each other for seven grueling games— Game 2 ended in a 6–6 tie after eleven innings—when they faced off for the finale on October 16.

The game went a full nine innings with the score tied, 1–1. The rowdy Boston crowd was hungry for a championship. In the top of the tenth, Snodgrass' teammate and fellow goat Fred Merkle (see separate chapter), smashed an RBI double off legendary Red Sox righty Smoky Joe Wood, putting the Giants ahead by one. That meant it was last call for the Red Sox. All the Giants had to do was retire the Sox and the championship was in the bag.

They ran into trouble, though. Wood had hurt his pitching hand barehanding a play on the final out and was taken out of the game. Pinch hitter Clyde Engle stood in for him to start the bottom of the tenth and hit a soft fly ball to center field. It looked to be the first out. Centerfielder

Snodgrass waved off the left fielder, got right under the ball, and dropped it. By the time Fred picked it up, Engle was standing calmly on second base, smiling at him.

Slugger Harry Hooper came up next and hit a screaming shot over Snodgrass' head. Racing back toward the wall with his back to the plate, Snodgrass snared the ball on the full run for the first out. He later called it the finest catch of his career. Engle, who was sure the ball was going for extra bases, barely got back to second safely. The next batter walked.

Tris Speaker came to bat with one out and two on. Giant pitcher Christy Mathewson got him to hit an easy foul-pop down the first base line. Fred Merkle was playing first and, for reasons still unknown, didn't even try to catch the ball. Witnesses say the ball almost landed in the coaching box—not even ten yards from Merkle. With new life, Speaker singled in the tying run. Moments later, after an intentional walk, the winning run came home on a sacrifice fly. After nine and a half tough innings, Boston won the deciding game on a couple of fluky plays. The papers dubbed Snodgrass the goat, ignoring both his amazing follow-up catch as well as Merkle's inexcusable lapse in failing to snare Speaker's foul.

Snodgrass played a few more years, but found himself frustrated by the fact that he was known only for dropping a fly. He left baseball at the age of 29. In *The Glory of Their Times*, which was written late in his life, Fred remembered his World Series error and its aftermath with a mixture of amusement and bitterness. ". . . According to the newspapers, Fred Snodgrass lost the World Series. I did drop that fly ball, and that did put what turned out to be the tying run on base, but that's a long way from 'losing a World Series.' However, the facts don't seem to matter."

The Verdict

Granted, Fred Snodgrass blew it. Since 1912, he never could offer an explanation for his missed fly. But imagine if he had caught the easy fly and missed the tough one; the Giants still would have lost the game and Series, yet no one would have blamed Snodgrass for not making a miraculous catch. And, as painful as it may be to admit, Fred Merkle—the Giants' other Fred—also deserves a heap of blame for the Series outcome. He didn't even make a go at Speaker's foul-pop.

George Steinbrenner
Owner
New York Yankees
1973–Present

In 1973, shipping magnate George Steinbrenner bought himself a baseball team. And not just any team: he copped the storied New York Yankees. It cost him $10 million, a sum he considered appropriate for a prestige purchase of this kind.

Prestige was, to hear him talk, all George had in mind. He never claimed to be a good front-office executive. Baseball was still trying to come to grips with one misguided would-be owner/manager, Charlie Finley. (See separate chapter on Finley and Mike Andrews.) It didn't need another one, and Steinbrenner seemed to sense this. He laughed off suggestions that he might try to actually *run* the Yankee organization: "I won't," he promised, "be involved in the day-to-day operations of the club at all."

Right. You have to give Steinbrenner his due. The Yankees, baseball's proudest franchise, had hit on hard times when he purchased them. Their last World Series victory had come in 1962, and they had developed a habit of finishing out of the money year after disappointing year. The glory years of Ruth, Gehrig, DiMaggio, and Mantle seemed far away. The proud Yankee tradition was something you read about in history books, not something you went to the ballpark to see. Steinbrenner resolved to buy himself a championship team, and, to his credit, it worked. For a while.

George's attitude could be summed up as follows: "If something's not working, throw money at it." There was certainly a positive side to this approach—namely the championship Yankee squads of 1977 and 1978, which boasted such high-priced superstar acquisitions as Reggie Jackson and Catfish Hunter. But there was a downside as well. For one thing, Steinbrenner's management of clubhouse relations and personnel issues showed a certain, shall we say, lack of consistency and tact. The morale was usually lousy, and problems that simmered unattended during the glory years came back to haunt the Bronx Bombers in leaner times.

Take managers, for instance; a representative sampling of comings and goings will give an idea of the revolving-door mentality that held sway during Steinbrenner's reign.

On July 25, 1978, Billy Martin was fired for having made reference to Steinbrenner's conviction for illegal campaign contributions to Richard Nixon. Bob Lemon replaced him, and the team went on to overtake the Boston Red Sox and win the World Series. Accordingly, he was fired early on in the 1979 season. Billy Martin was then rehired, but was fired again at the end of the season. Dick Howser took the reins and lasted a whole year, guiding the Yanks to a 103–59 season, their best since 1963. But Steinbrenner wanted a championship, and Howser was canned after the Yankees fell to the underdog Royals in the American League Championship Series. Gene Michael was named the new manager in November 1980; he didn't make it to the end of the next season, and was replaced by Bob Lemon, who, you will remember, had been fired back in '79. Lemon barely made it out of spring training in '82, and was fired for the second time in a little over three years on April 25. Then Gene Michael took the helm again, and . . .

You get the idea. George made some, well, *impulsive* personnel changes (Martin, for instance, was hired and fired five times). And they weren't restricted to managers. The list of players benched (and even sent down to the minors) on Steinbrenner's orders as a result of errant play is too long to include here. Such tactics made for good media fodder when they could be backed up with results on the field. Unfortunately for Yankee fans, the last Bronx Bomber Squad to appear in a World Series was, an undistinguished 1981 entry that benefited heavily from the erratic dictates of the commissioner's office on the postseason playoff structure necessitated by the strike season. The Yankees lost.

Need more evidence? How about blackmailing players and cavorting with gamblers? Steinbrenner managed both of these in one go, and the subsequent Dave Winfield-Howie Spira mess got so sordid that the owner was eventually barred from the day-to-day operations of his team, an unprecedented move.

George Steinbrenner was—and, as of this writing, still is—a thorn in the side of Yankee fans everywhere. He won a couple of championships, for which he deserves full credit. He also helped throw baseball's salary structure completely out of balance, made a mockery of the proudest franchise in the history of sport, and generally acted like the jerk he is at every possible opportunity. Sound harsh? It's meant to. Let's remember that we're talking about the man who made Yogi Berra swear never to set foot inside Yankee Stadium until new owners took over.

Yogi's said a lot of dumb things in his day. That wasn't one of them.

The Verdict

Why does George Steinbrenner belong in this book? There are any number of incidents to point to; most sportwriters tended to lump them all together. A typical response claimed that George merited goathood simply "for being George Steinbrenner." We're inclined to agree with the sentiment. We also note that the Yankee owner racked up the most votes of any non-player in our poll, beating out such luminaries as Harry Frazee and Charlie Finley.

Ralph Terry
Pitcher, New York Yankees
World Series *vs.* Pittsburgh Pirates
October 13, 1960

YEAR	TEAM	W	L	G	GS	IP	H	HR	BB	SO	ERA
1956	Yankees	1	2	3	3	13	17	2	11	8	9.69
1957	Yankees	1	1	7	2	21	18	1	8	7	3.00
1957	Athletics	4	11	21	19	131	119	15	47	80	3.37
1958	Athletics	11	13	40	33	217	217	29	61	134	4.23
1959	Athletics	2	4	9	7	46	56	9	19	35	5.28
1959	Yankees	3	7	24	16	127	130	7	30	55	3.40
1960	Yankees	10	8	35	23	167	149	15	52	92	3.40
1961	Yankees	16	3	31	27	188	162	19	42	86	3.16
1962	Yankees	23	12	43	39	299	257	40	57	176	3.19
1963	Yankees	17	15	40	37	268	246	29	39	114	3.22
1964	Yankees	7	11	27	14	115	130	20	31	77	4.54
1965	Indians	11	6	30	26	166	154	22	23	84	3.69
1966	Athletics	1	5	15	10	64	65	7	15	33	3.80
1966	Mets	0	1	11	1	25	27	1	11	14	4.68
1967	Mets	0	0	2	0	3	1	0	0	5	0.00
	CAREER TOTALS	107	99	338	257	1850	1748	216	446	1000	3.62

It's become part of American tradition for fathers to play ball with their kids and say something like, "Okay, son. It's the final game of the World Series. Bottom of the ninth and the score's tied. Here's the pitch . . ." It's purely hypothetical; it just doesn't seem to happen that much in the major leagues. But on October 13, 1960, New York Yankee pitcher Ralph Terry was in that very situation—and the way it came out probably wasn't the culmination of Terry's sandlot fantasies.

The 1960 World Series between the favored New York Yankees and the underdog Pittsburgh Pirates was absurd in many ways. Statistically speaking, New York should have cremated Pittsburgh. Over seven games, the Yankees: batted .338, a World Series record, compared to the Bucs' paltry .256; scored 55 runs against the Pirates' 27; and had an ERA of 3.54 that was quite respectable next to Pittsburgh's obese 7.11. The Yanks put up all these numbers, but lost the championship.

In Pittsburgh, the Pirates started things off by winning Game 1, 6–4. But the Yanks shook off the cobwebs and clobbered the Pirates in the next two games by scores of 16–3 and 10–0. Game 4 was a pitchers' duel, finally going to Pittsburgh, 3–2. Ralph Terry took the loss, giving up all three Pirate runs in the fifth inning. The Pirates took Game 5, 5–2, and the Yankees won Game 6, 12–0, behind the masterful pitching of future Hall of Famer Whitey Ford.

The series was tied at three games apiece, and a championship-deciding seventh game would be played at Pittsburgh's Forbes Field. For all of their batting and pitching heroics, the Yankees now found themselves back at square one. They had to shut down the pesky Pirates one last time.

The Pirates jumped on the board first, scoring two runs in each of the first two innings. In the fifth and sixth innings, however, New York scored five times to go up, 5–4. They made it 7–4 in the top of the eighth and it looked like Casey Stengel's Yankees would take home their eighth World Series title in ten years.

But things got a little weird in the bottom of the eighth. Two singles, a freak bad-hop grounder off of Yankee shortstop Tony Kubek's throat, an infield hit, and a Hal Smith home run resulted in five Pirate runs. Kubek was taken out of the game and had to be hospitalized. The score was now 9–7, Pittsburgh.

If the eighth inning was weird, the ninth was downright surreal. Before the New York half was over, the Yanks had combined three singles with a ground out to bring the score to 9–9.

It was every kid's dream situation: a tie ballgame in the bottom of the ninth inning of the seventh game of the World Series. Terry was on the mound for New York, needing three quick outs to keep his team alive and send the game into extra innings. Bill Mazeroski was the first Pirate to step up to the plate. Terry missed with the first pitch. His second was a chest-high fastball—just what Bill was looking for. Maz swung and launched the ball into the left-centerfield stands to win the game. It marked the first (and, so far, only) time a World Series had been decided by a home run in the bottom of the ninth inning.

After Maz' blast, there was pandemonium on the field. Fans poured onto the diamond and mobbed the jubilant Mazeroski—who almost didn't reach home plate. But the run scored, the Pirates won, and Mazeroski had won his place in history. So, for that matter, had Terry.

The Verdict

After the game, someone approached the dejected Terry and asked him what pitch he had delivered to Mazeroski. Terry's glum—and accurate—reply: "The wrong one."

George Bell

Toronto Blue Jays
1987 season finish

The Toronto Blue Jays were sinking fast. Literally. Their charter flight from Toronto to Detroit, where they would take on the second-place Tigers for the final series of the regular season, was on fire. One of the engines had burst into flames when it sucked in a passing bird, and now the team plane was forced to make an emergency landing. "The bird was not an albatross," sportswriter Peter Gammons would later observe, "but it might as well have been."

The Jays had held a 3½-game lead with only one week to play. Now the Tigers had crept back into the race, trailing by only a single game, and they would play Toronto three times before capacity Tiger Stadium crowds. The three games to come—featuring the teams with the two best records in baseball—would test the mettle of the Toronto outfit, which had taken much hometown criticism in recent years. Fans knocked Toronto for dropping the 1985 American League Championship Series to the underdog Royals, and for failing in a late-season effort to overtake the Red Sox in 1986. With the Tigers closing fast, would the Blue Jays finally be able to win the big games this year?

If the first game in Detroit was any indication, the Toronto faithful were not going to like the answer to that question. A suddenly porous Blue Jay defense allowed the Tigers four outs instead of the customary three in the second inning. And the third. And the fourth. And the fifth. And the sixth. Add to that the fact that slugger George Bell was in an RBI slump, and you had a 4–3 Tiger victory. The two teams were in a dead heat for first place.

The second game was a pitcher's duel between the Tigers' Jack Morris and Toronto's Mike Flanagan. Toronto took a 2–1 lead in the fifth, but then

Detroit evened things up late in the game and sent the contest into extra innings. By then, rookie Jeff Musselman had taken the mound for Toronto; Musselman had been asked to warm up a total of six times during the game—and it showed. When the rookie loaded up the bases in the twelfth, Blue Jay manager Jimmy Williams called not for ace stopper Tom Henke, but for sophomore reliever Mark Eichhorn. Eichhorn promptly yielded a single to Alan Trammell, and the once-confident Jays trailed the Tigers by a game.

That put everything on the line for the final regularly scheduled game of the season. Toronto had to beat Detroit's Frank Tanana in order to force a one-game playoff to decide the division winner. There was only one problem: Tanana (who was 5–1 as a Tiger against Toronto for his career) was essentially unhittable. Going into the eighth, he held a 1–0 lead and looked like a man on a mission. With a man on, Tanana retired Bell (whose RBI slump was now reaching epic proportions) to defuse the last Toronto rally of the season.

The Jays could not score in the ninth, either. End of game. End of pennant race. End of dream. "I'm dreading going home," confessed Toronto pitcher John Cerruti. "The first person I see is gonna ask, 'What happened?'"

The Verdict

The Blue Jays, like their rivals/kindred spirits the Boston Red Sox, have a justly earned reputation for choking in the big games, and pennant-race games don't get much bigger than the three-game showdown in Tiger Stadium at the end of the '87 season. It gets worse: We can now add to the legacy of Toronto frustration ALCS losses in 1989 and 1991.

Hardly a spring goes by that does not see the Toronto club anointed early on as the league's "best club on paper" and "the team to beat in the East." And, to their credit, usually they *are* the team to beat. So far, though, someone's always dutifully gone out and beaten the Blue Jays whenever they've shown the faintest glimmerings of postseason potential.

Mike Torrez
Pitcher, Boston Red Sox
A.L. East Divisional Playoff *vs.* New York Yankees
October 2, 1978

CAREER HIGHLIGHTS

YEAR	TEAM	W	L	G	GS	IP	H	HR	BB	SO	ERA
1972	Expos	16	12	34	33	243	215	15	103	112	3.33
1973	Expos	9	12	35	34	208	207	17	115	90	4.46
1974	Expos	15	8	32	30	186	184	10	84	92	3.58
1975	Orioles	20	9	36	36	271	238	15	133	119	3.06
1976	A's	16	12	39	39	266	231	15	87	115	2.50
1977	A's	3	1	4	4	26	23	3	11	12	4.50
1977	Yankees	14	12	31	31	217	212	20	75	90	3.82
1978	Red Sox	16	13	36	36	250	272	19	99	120	3.96
1979	Red Sox	16	13	36	36	252	254	20	121	125	4.50
1980	Red Sox	9	16	36	32	207	256	18	75	97	5.09
1981	Red Sox	10	3	22	22	127	130	10	51	54	3.69
1982	Red Sox	9	9	31	31	176	196	20	74	84	5.22
	CAREER TOTALS	185	160	494	458	3042	3043	223	1371	1404	3.96

After blowing a July 20th nine-game lead in the American League East (see separate chapter), the 1978 Boston Red Sox got hot again in late September. They won twelve of their last fourteen games to wind up in a dramatic first place tie with arch-rivals the New York Yankees.

Although they had amazing power throughout the lineup—number nine hitter Butch Hobson hit 30 homers in 1977 and 17 in 1978—the '78 Red Sox were somewhat weak in the pitching department. Thirty-two-year-old Mike Torrez, whom the Red Sox acquired as a free agent from the Yankees the year before, had a tremendous first half-season, followed by a month and a half in which he proved incapable of winning a game. When the Sox got hot in September, Torrez found his stuff and was just about up to his first-half level. In the one-game playoff, he was matched against the virtually unhittable Ron Guidry, who was winding up a record-breaking 24–3 (soon to be 25–3) season.

The Sox got to Guidry early in this game. Left fielder Carl Yastrzemski, who simply could not hit Guidry during the season, surprised everyone when he uncorked a line-drive homer in the bottom of the second to put the Sox on the board first. They added another run in the sixth on Jim Rice's RBI single. Then with two on and two out, Fred Lynn ripped a scorcher down the right field line for what appeared to be a sure two-run double. The double was not meant to be. Yankee right fielder Lou Piniella was playing twenty yards out of his usual position and handily caught the liner for the last out. Piniella admitted it was a gamble, but said he just had a hunch Lynn would pull the ball.

Torrez wasn't too worried. He was holding his own. His team was ahead 2–0 with just three more innings to go. Then with two on and two out in the top of the seventh, up stepped one Bucky Dent. Not known for his power, Dent was, at this stage, the proud possessor of 22 lifetime homers in over 2,600 lifetime at bats. He fouled the second pitch off his foot and jumped around in pain. While the trainer attended to him, teammate Mickey Rivers noticed that Dent's bat was slightly cracked and he grabbed a new one for him.

During the moments that Dent was being treated, Torrez did not throw any warm up pitches. Later, he remembered, "I didn't throw . . . I should have thrown a couple to get myself back . . . I didn't realize it was going to be four or five minutes. I thought he was going to get another bat and get back in."

Dent settled back into the box armed with his new bat and cortisone-treated foot. Torrez, cold after spending five minutes watching the infielders play round-the-horn, delivered a meatball just as the wind shifted out to left field. Dent swatted at it and hit a pop fly to left. At least it looked like a pop fly to everyone in the ballpark.

Boston catcher Carlton Fisk said, "After he hit it I let out a sigh of relief. I thought, 'We got away with that mistake pitch.' Then I saw Yaz looking up and said, 'Oh God.'" The ball didn't come down. It just rode the wind and came to rest in the netting over Fenway Park's "Green Monster" for a three-run homer.

That pop-fly home run was all the Yanks needed: they hung on to win the game, the pennant, and the World Series. Torrez didn't get off the hook in Boston until 1986 (see chapters on Bill Buckner and Calvin Schiraldi/ Bob Stanley).

The Verdict

Torrez pitched a decent game. Okay, so he forgot to stay loose during a delay and had the misfortune to pitch to Dent just as the wind shifted. This does not necessarily make a goat. The real goat of the 1978 season was the Red Sox team for blowing a 13½-game lead. There never should have been a playoff game in the first place. See "1978 Boston Red Sox" chapter for the gory details.

Ted Williams
Outfield, Boston Red Sox
World Series *vs.* St. Louis Cardinals
October 1–15, 1946

CAREER HIGHLIGHTS

YEAR	TEAM	AVG	G	AB	R	H	2B	3B	HR	RBI
1939	Red Sox	.327	149	565	131	185	44	11	31	145
1940	Red Sox	.344	144	561	134	193	43	14	23	113
1941	Red Sox	.406	143	456	135	185	33	3	37	120
1942	Red Sox	.356	150	522	141	186	34	5	36	137
1946	Red Sox	.342	150	514	142	176	37	8	38	123
1947	Red Sox	.343	156	528	125	181	40	9	32	114
1948	Red Sox	.369	137	509	124	188	44	3	25	127
1949	Red Sox	.343	155	566	150	194	39	3	43	159
1951	Red Sox	.318	148	531	109	169	28	4	30	126
1955	Red Sox	.356	98	320	77	114	21	3	28	83
1957	Red Sox	.388	132	420	96	163	28	1	38	87
	CAREER TOTALS	.344	2292	7706	1798	2654	525	71	521	1839

After decades in the second division, the Red Sox finally brought exciting baseball back to Boston in the 1940s. Led by Ted Williams (.342, 38, 123), the 1946 Sox ran away with the American League pennant. They won 104 games and Williams was named American League MVP.

In the National League, the St. Louis Cardinals had a tougher time at it. In fact, they ended the regular season in a first-place tie with the Brooklyn Dodgers, forcing baseball's first pennant-deciding playoff series. The Cards struggled but pulled off the mini-series, two games to one.

Meanwhile, Red Sox manager Joe Cronin was concerned that his team would lose its sharpness during the four-day delay created by the National League mini-series. He decided to keep his players honed by staging three exhibition games pitting the Sox against an American League All-Star team. As fate would have it, Ted Williams was hit on the elbow by a pitch in the first of these games. Williams said he was fine, but he was conspicuously absent from the rest of the exhibition series.

The World Series got under way with Williams back in the lineup. It was a see-saw series, with each team winning alternately until the seventh and deciding game. Throughout the series, Williams' bat was uncharacteristically silent. He managed only five hits, one of them a bunt single—something the Splendid Splinter rarely lowered himself to. As the cleanup hitter, he knocked in only one run. For a man who struck out a microscopic 44 times during the regular season, Williams raised some eyebrows when he led his team with five whiffs in the 1946 World Series.

The Cardinals took the last game 4–3 on Enos Slaughter's mad dash from first to home in the eighth. Johnny Pesky, who slightly delayed his throw to the plate, was labeled the series goat after declaring "I'm the goat!" in front of a room full of reporters (see chapter on Pesky). But because of his pitiful World Series performance, many feel Williams really deserves the designation.

After the Series, it was clear that Williams felt terrible about his lack of production. But he never made excuses, although he said little to the press. He gave his World Series share of over $2,000 to the batboy.

The Verdict

It is impossible to know exactly how much Williams' injured elbow affected his swing in the World Series, but it seems fair to say that the Kid was not at the top of his game. How else does one explain his decision to resort to bunting? Considering the closeness of the '46 Series, Williams' poor performance takes on special significance. If Williams had squeezed out a performance more on a level with his regular season, it's a good bet that the championship would have gone to Boston.

Lewis "Hack" Wilson
Outfield, Chicago Cubs
World Series vs. Philadelphia Athletics
October 12, 1929

YEAR	TEAM	AVG	G	AB	R	H	2B	3B	HR	RBI
1923	Giants	.200	3	10	0	2	0	0	0	0
1924	Giants	.295	107	383	62	113	19	12	10	57
1925	Giants	.239	62	180	28	43	7	4	6	30
1926	Cubs	.321	142	529	97	170	36	8	21	109
1927	Cubs	.318	146	551	119	175	30	12	30	129
1928	Cubs	.313	145	520	89	163	32	9	31	120
1929	Cubs	.345	150	574	135	198	30	5	39	159
1930	Cubs	.356	155	585	146	208	35	6	56	190
1931	Cubs	.261	112	395	66	103	22	4	13	61
1932	Dodgers	.297	135	481	77	143	37	5	23	123
1933	Dodgers	.267	117	360	41	96	13	2	9	54
1934	Dodgers	.262	67	172	24	45	5	0	6	27
1934	Phillies	.100	7	20	0	2	0	0	0	3
	CAREER TOTALS	.307	1348	4760	884	1461	266	67	244	1062

Standing five feet six and weighing over 200 pounds, Hack Wilson was unusual-looking as far as professional athletes go. Despite his proportions, Hack was one of the premier hitters of his time.

But it was in 1929 that Wilson helped his team, the Chicago Cubs, blow the biggest, latest lead in World Series history and earned himself a place among the all-time goats of the game.

The Philadelphia Athletics of 1929 hit .296 as a team—absurdly high by today's standards—and boasted legendary names up and down the roster. Jimmie Foxx led the league with a .463 on-base percentage and smacked 33 dingers. Mickey Cochrane hit .331 while earning the reputation of one of the game's premier catchers. And Lefty Grove was a handy guy to have on the staff; he won twenty, led the league with 170 strikeouts, and wound up in the Hall of Fame.

With the A's winning the 1929 AL pennant easily, life was good for Philadelphians. But over in Chicago, Rogers Hornsby, Kiki Cuyler, and Hack Wilson were playing some mean ball, too. The A's may have hit .296 as a team, but the Windy City's Cubs batted .303. (You could really get some offense going in the late twenties and early thirties.) The league leader charts were peppered with Chicago players at season's end, and experts were predicting an evenly matched World Series.

In Chicago, the A's took the first two games of the best-of-seven series by scores of 3–1 and 9–3, respectively. The series moved to Philadelphia's Shibe Park, where the Cubs continued the home field-disadvantage trend by edging the A's 3–1. The Athletics still had a two-games-to-one edge, but the Cubs seemed to be catching up.

Game 4 proved to be the turning point of the World Series. Chicago ace Charlie Root was on fire, and the Cubs seemed poised to tie the series at two games apiece, holding a more-than-comfortable 8–0 lead going into the bottom of the seventh inning.

A's manager Connie Mack had all but given up, deciding to pull his regulars after one more inning. He was filling out a new line-up card with bench-warmers' names when Al Simmons hit a solo homer to make it 8–1. Root then gave up six consecutive singles and the A's deficit had been whittled to just four runs. Mack tore up the new line-up card.

With two men on, Root was relieved by Art Nehf, who would deal to outfielder Mule Haas (not to be confused with *Moose* Haas, who came along much later). Haas banged a liner right at Hack Wilson in center. Without moving, Wilson could have nabbed it to kill the rally. Instead, he lost the ball in the sun and ducked as it sailed past him and rolled toward the fence. Before Kiki Cuyler could retrieve the ball, Haas had huffed and puffed around the diamond for a three-run inside-the-park homer. Shibe Park exploded.

The Cubs were still leading, 8–7, but that wouldn't last long. Philadelphia roughed up two more Chicago hurlers for an additional three runs before the inning was over. When it did finally end, the score stood at 10–8. Lefty Grove came in from the bullpen and retired the final six Cubs in a row—four of them on strikeouts. The A's had scored an unprecedented ten runs in one inning of a World Series game to win Game 4 and take a 3–1 lead in games.

The A's secured the championship in a dramatic come-from-behind bottom of the ninth inning of the next game. After what transpired in Game 4, however, the final game was an anticlimax.

Cynics labeled Wilson the man who lost the World Series for Chicago. It was conveniently forgotten that he'd led the Cubs with a .471 Series average. However, more charitable souls penned "Wrigley Field Blues", a song that paid tribute to Hack and the unfortunate Cubs. The opening line was, "The sun shone bright in our great Hack Wilson's eyes . . ."

Wilson soon forgot about his goat status; the following year the future Hall of Famer hit .356 and set the major league standard for runs batted in with an astounding total of 190.

The Verdict

Old Hack wasn't so much a goat as a victim of natural circumstances. As in the case of Willie Davis in 1966 (see separate chapter), Hack Wilson lost a fly ball in the sun. Unfortunately for him, this occurred at the worst possible time: in the middle of a record-setting rally. Let the record show, too, that it takes more than one man to whittle an eight-run lead down to one run in a single inning.

SPECIAL LAST-MINUTE GOAT

Lonnie Smith
Outfielder, Atlanta Braves
1991 World Series, Game 7

With no score in the eighth inning of Game 7 of the 1991 World Series against the Minnesota Twins, the Braves' Terry Pendleton hit a shot to the gap in left center. Lonnie Smith, who was on first and running on the pitch, lost the ball and hesitated at second base. When he realized the ball was still being chased down, he headed for third base. Smith was safe at third, but should have easily scored what would have been the winning run. The Twins got out of the jam unscathed and won the game, 1–0, in the tenth inning. Smith's running error proved to cost the game and championship.

Lonnie Smith didn't get many votes because our survey was distributed before the '91 World Series. The few surveys that came in after the Series, however, *all* nominated Smith. It will be interesting to see how history treats him.

Honorable Mention

Our survey was sent to over 600 sports journalists across the country and yielded close to a 50% response rate. What follows is an alphabetical list of the various baseball players, managers, executives, and others who received an all-time goat nomination, but did not garner enough votes to merit a full chapter:

Joaquin Andujar, St. Louis Cardinals pitcher: Disastrous unraveling in 1985 World Series; destroyed locker room after Game 7.

Artificial Turf Inventor: Self-explanatory.

1969 Atlanta Braves: Choked in first N.L. playoffs vs. New York Mets.

Gene Autry, California Angels owner: Was consistently foolish in free agent signings; big contracts, no winners.

1969 Baltimore Orioles: Lost the World Series to 100-1 longshot New York Mets.

Roseanne Barr, television actress: Butchered National Anthem at a 1990 Padres game.

Buzzie Bavasi, California Angels general manager: Let Nolan Ryan get away in 1979. In justifying his decision Bavasi said, "We'll just go get a couple of 8-7 pitchers."

Albert Belle, Cleveland Indians outfielder: Threw a ball at a fan in a 1991 rage.

Bingo Binks, Washington Senators outfielder: With the 1945 A.L. pennant on the line, Binks dropped an easy fly ball. He had forgotten to put on his eyeglasses.

Donie Bush, Pittsburgh Pirate manager: Kept Pirate star Kiki Cuyler out of the 1927 World Series because of a fued between the two. Yankees swept the Pirates in four games.

Al Campanis, Los Angeles Dodgers executive: Made racist remarks, saying blacks ". . . lack the necessities . . ." to hold management jobs. Lost *his* job as a result.

Hugh Casey, Brooklyn Dodgers pitcher: Either threw a spitball or crossed up signs with catcher Mickey Owen in 1941 World Series against the New York Yankees.

Pitch went for a third strike/passed ball, igniting a rally and setting the stage for a Yankee world championship. (See chapter on Mickey Owen.)

The Mighty Casey, Mudville Nine outfielder: Struck out.

Jack Chesbro, New York Yankees pitcher: His wild pitch late in the 1904 season gave the A.L. flag to Boston.

Vince Coleman, St. Louis Cardinals outfielder: Got caught in the tarp in the 1985 N.L. playoffs.

Charlie Comiskey, Chicago White Sox owner: It has been argued that, because of his stinginess, he compelled his players to embark on the 1919 "Black Sox" World Series scandal (see separate chapter).

Howard Cosell, sports broadcaster: Had "no business" covering baseball.

Tony Cuccinello, Chicago White Sox third base coach: Sent slow-footed Sherm Lollar home in Game 2 of 1959 World Series against the L.A. Dodgers. Lollar, representing the tying run, was nailed easily at the plate and the Sox lost the Series in six tight games.

Pat Darcy, Cincinnati Reds pitcher: Gave up dramatic Carlton Fisk homer in Game 6 of 1975 World Series.

Dick Drago/Jack Billingham: These two Boston Red Sox pitchers gave up three home runs to California Angel Freddie Patek in a 1980 game. Patek retired with 41 lifetime home runs in 5,530 at bats.

Curt Flood, St. Louis Cardinals outfielder: Was picked off at a key moment in Game 7 of the 1968 World Series. The Cardinals ended up losing the series to the Tigers. (See chapter on Lou Brock.)

Jim Frey, Kansas City Royals manager: During the 1980 World Series, he lifted Larry Gura in the seventh inning of Games 2 and 5. In both cases, Gura had a three-hitter going against the Phillies, who came back to win each game as well as the Series.

Ford Frick, commissioner: Tarnished Roger Maris' single-season home run mark in 1961 by qualifying it as representing the 162-game record.

Goose Goslin, Detroit Tigers outfielder: Hit into four double plays in one game in 1934.

Hank Gowdy, New York Giants catcher: Tripped on his mask and missed foul-pop in Game 7 of 1924 World Series vs. Washington Senators. With new life, the batter cracked a double and the Senators won the championship.

Mike Grady, Philadelphia Phillies catcher: Committed four errors on a single play in 1895.

M. Donald Grant, New York Mets executive: In 1977, he let Mets stars Dave Kingman and Tom Seaver get away without rhyme, reason or adequate compensation for the Mets.

Calvin Griffith, Washington Senators owner: With his team going broke, he was given the opportunity to move them to Los Angeles. He responded, "Los Angeles isn't ready for major league baseball." The Dodgers have managed to draw a fan or two to Chavez Ravine. The Senators no longer exist.

Gil Hodges, Brooklyn Dodgers first baseman: Went 0-for-21 in the seven games of the 1952 World Series.

John Holland, Chicago Cubs general manager: Traded Lou Brock for the immortal Ernie Broglio.

Chuck Hostetler, Chicago Cubs pinch hitter: In 1945 World Series vs. Detroit Tigers, he fell down between third and home, costing the Cubs a run and the game.

Darrell Johnson, Boston Red Sox manager: Didn't replace questionable pitcher Jim Burton in Game 7 of the 1975 World Series. Red Sox lost championship by one run.

Mark Koenig, New York Yankees shortstop: His key error helped lose the 1926 Series to the Cardinals.

Judge Kenesaw Mountain Landis, commissioner: Steadfastly denied blacks the opportunity to play major league baseball. He never offered a reason beyond euphemistic references to "gentlemen's agreements."

Frank Lane, Cleveland Indians general manager: Traded Rocky Colavito for Harvey Kuenn in 1960. Indians haven't contended since.

Mark Littell, Kansas City Royals pitcher: Gave up dramatic pennant-winning home run to Yankee Chris Chambliss in 1976 A.L. Playoffs.

Ernie Lombardi, Cincinnati Reds catcher: Sat dazed in the backstop dirt while two runs scored in the 1939 World Series.

Gary Lucas, California Angels pitcher: Hit Rich Gedman in Game 5 of 1986 A.L. playoffs, setting the stage for Dave Henderson's heroics. (See chapter on Donnie Moore.)

Steve Lyons, Boston Red Sox infielder: In the heat of the 1985 pennant race, his team down by a run, Lyons inexplicably tried to steal third with two outs in bottom of ninth with Wade Boggs at bat. He was out.

Denny McLain, pitcher for various teams including '68 Tiger squad: Gambling and various other shady dealings ruined his chances for a legendary career.

Cal McLish, Cleveland Indians pitcher: Served up four homers in one inning of a 1956 game.

John McMullen, Houston Astros owner: Let Nolan Ryan get away in 1988.

John McNamara, Boston Red Sox manager: Could have replaced the hobbled Bill Buckner with Don Baylor or Dave Stapleton at first base in 1986 World Series. Instead, he chose to stick with Buckner—the rest is history. (See chapters on Bill Buckner and Calvin Schiraldi/Bob Stanley.)

Mario Mendoza, utilityman for several teams: Retired with a lifetime batting average of .215. Prompted the widely-used term "The Mendoza Line."

Clarence Mitchell, Brooklyn Robins pitcher: In two consecutive at bats in the 1920 World Series vs. Cleveland, Mitchell hit into a double play and a triple play, respectively. The Indians won the Series, five games to two.

Gaylord Perry, pitcher for various teams: Admitted throwing spitballs; snuck under the wire into the Hall of Fame.

Pete Rose: Gambling, gambling, gambling.

Bob Scheffing, New York Mets executive: Traded Nolan Ryan to the Angels for Jim Fregosi in 1971.

Seattle Pilots/Mariners: 20-plus years of sub .500 ballplaying in the Puget Sound region. As of this writing, Florida beckons.

Marv Throneberry, New York Mets first baseman: "Mr. Met" (see 1962 New York Mets chapter).

Bob Tolan, Cincinnati Reds outfielder: His three-base error in the seventh game of the 1972 World Series led to a costly run; the A's won the game and championship, 3–2.

Ted Turner, Atlanta Braves owner: After firing manager Dave Bristol, Turner donned a uniform and tried to manage the Braves for a game. He lost.

Peter Ueberroth, commissioner: "The Collusion Commissioner."

Bill Veeck, St. Louis Browns and Chicago White Sox owner: Masterminded a variety of embarrassing publicity stunts including: Eddie Gaedel, the pinch-hitting midget; Disco Demolition Night; and the infamous exploding scoreboard.

Fred "Fireball" Wenz, Boston Red Sox pitcher: In a 1969 game against the laughable Seattle Pilots, Wenz gave up successive homers to Larry Haney, pitcher Mike Marshall, and Ray Oyler. The three batters combined to hit 28 lifetime homers in almost 2,500 major league at bats.

Stan Williams, Los Angeles Dodgers pitcher: Walked in winning run of 1962 playoffs vs. San Francisco Giants.

Willie Wilson, Kansas City Royals outfielder: During the 1980 World Series, Wilson struck out a record twelve times, including the final out of the final game.

Dave Winfield, New York Yankees outfielder: Went 1 for 21 in the 1981 World Series. Also engaged in shady financial dealings with Winfield Foundation funds.

George Wright, Texas Rangers outfielder: In an important game against the Red Sox, Wright threw the ball into the dugout, allowing the winning Boston runs to score after the two runners had slid into second base from different directions.

Heinie Zimmerman, New York Giants third baseman: Chased Eddie Collins across the plate for the winning run in a botched rundown attempt in the final game of the 1917 World Series vs. Chicago White Sox.

The Survey Results

The following chart displays the ranking of the top forty-one goats according to our survey. The "percentage" figure reflects the percentage of surveys that made mention of that particular goat. Hence, if ten journalists returned surveys, and the goat was mentioned in all ten, his percentage would be 100.

RANK	NAME	PERCENTAGE
1	Bill Buckner	86%
2	Ralph Branca	63%
3	Fred Merkle	59%
4	Mickey Owen	55%
5	1964 Philadelphia Phillies	41%
6	George Steinbrenner	31%
7	Charlie Finley/Mike Andrews	28%
8	Gene Mauch	26%
9	Don Denkinger	24%
9	Harry Frazee	24%
11	Johnny Pesky	22%
12	Ralph Terry	21%
13	Mike Torrez	20%
14	1919 Chicago White Sox	18%
15	Leo Durocher/1969 Chicago Cubs	17%
15	Dennis Eckersley	17%
17	Fred Snodgrass	16%
18	Leon Durham	14%

18	Donnie Moore	14%
20	1978 Boston Red Sox	12%
20	Tom Lasorda	12%
20	1987 Toronto Blue Jays	12%
23	1951 Brooklyn Dodgers	11%
24	Roger Clemens	8%
24	Bob Moose	8%
24	1990 Oakland A's	8%
24	Babe Ruth	8%
28	Cap Anson	7%
28	Jose Canseco	7%
28	1954 Cleveland Indians	7%
28	Willie Davis	7%
28	1962 New York Mets	7%
28	Roger Peckinpaugh	7%
34	Calvin Shiraldi/Bob Stanley	5%
34	Ted Williams	5%
36	Lou Brock	4%
36	Joe McCarthy	4%
36	Tom Niedenfuer	4%
36	Hack Wilson	4%
40	Larry Barnett	3%
40	Jerry Dybzinski	3%

Sportswriters' Credits

This book would not have been possible without all the good people who took time out of their busy day to fill out a "goat survey." Once again, thanks everyone.

Here is a listing of sports journalists who participated in the survey:

Dave Anderson, *New York Times*
Kent Baker, *Baltimore Sun*
Rod Beaton, *USA Today*
Harland Beery, *Bremerton Sun*
Steve Bisheff, *Orange County Register*
Furman Bisher, *Atlanta Journal*
Hal Bock, *Associated Press*
Stephen Bray
Bob Brookover
Pete Cava, freelance
Rich Chere, *Star-Ledger*
Ritter Collett, *Dayton Daily News*
Dave Cunningham, *Long Beach Press-Telegram*
Dave D'Alessandro, *The National*
Rick Davis, *San Diego Tribune*
Tony DeMarco, *Fort Worth Star-Telegram*
Rob Dewolf, *The Repository*
Dick Draper, *San Mateo Times*
Jay Dunn, *The Trentonian*
Mel Durslag
Jack Etkin, *Kansas City Star*
Mark Fainaru, freelance
Ray Finocchiaro, *Wilmington News Journal*
Bud Geracie, *San Jose Mercury News*
Alan Goldstein, *Baltimore Sun*
Kenny Hand, *Houston Post*
Tom Haudricourt, *Milwaukee Sentinel*

Gregg Hoffmann, *Kenosha News*
Jeff Horrigan, *The National*
Alan Hoskins, *Kansas City Kansan*
Dan Hruby, *San Jose Mercury News*
Bob Hunter, *Los Angeles Daily News*
Joe Illuzzi, *New York Post*
Steve Jacobson, *New York Newsday*
Bruce Jenkins, *San Francisco Chronicle*
Moss Klein, *Star-Ledger*
Rob Kroichick, *Sacramento Bee*
Bob Kuenster, *Baseball Digest*
Mark Langill, *Pasadena Star-News*
Jack Lang, *SportsTicker*
Keith Langlois, *The Oakland Press*
Jim Lazar, *Salem News*
Bill Livingston, *Cleveland Plain Dealer*
Bill Lyon, *Philadelphia Inquirer*
Rich Marazzi, author/freelance
Jody McDonald, *WIP radio, Philadelphia*
Fred McMane, *United Press International*
Steve Meyerhoff, *The Sporting News*
Terence Moore, *Atlanta Journal-Constitution*
Larry O'Rourke, *North Jersey Herald & News*
John Perrotto, *Beaver County Times*
Gary Peterson, *Contra Costa Times*
Ron Rapoport, *Los Angeles Daily News*
Phil Rogers, *Dallas Times Herald*
Charlie Scoggins, *The Lowell Sun*
Dan Shaughnessy, *Boston Globe*
Mike Sheridan, *Baseball Bulletin*
Alan Solomon, *Chicago Tribune*
T.R. Sullivan, *Forth Worth Star Telegram*
Bill Tanton, *Baltimore Evening Sun*
Bob Valli, *The Oakland Tribune*
Juan Vene
Tom Verducci, *New York Newsday*
Vic Ziegel, *New York Daily News*

Note: There were numerous sportswriters who requested anonymity.

Bibliography

Boston Globe newspaper articles, 1978–1991.

Boston Herald newspaper articles, 1989–1991.

John Devaney and Burt Goldblatt. *The World Series*. Rand McNally & Co., 1972.

Glenn Dickey. *The History of the World Series*. Stein and Day, Inc., 1984.

Peter Gammons. *Beyond the Sixth Game*. Houghton Mifflin, 1985.

David Halberstam. *Summer of '49*. William Morrow, 1989.

Bill Madden and Moss Klein. *Damned Yankees*. Warner Books, 1990.

New York Times newspaper articles, 1925-1985.

Daniel Okrent and Steve Wulf. *Baseball Anecdotes*. Oxford University Press, 1989.

Dan Riley, ed. *The Red Sox Reader*, Revised Edition. Houghton Mifflin, 1991.

Lawrence Ritter. *The Glory of Their Times*. Macmillan, 1966.

George Robinson and Charles Salzberg. *On a Clear Day They Could See Seventh Place*. Dell Publishing, 1991.

Rutledge Books, Inc., eds. *This Great Game*. Prentice Hall, Inc., 1971.

Dan Shaughnessy. *The Curse of the Bambino*. Penguin Books, 1991.

— *One Strike Away*. Beaufort Books, 1987.

Sports Illustrated magazine articles, 1968-1990.

Rick Talley. *The Cubs of '69*. Contemporary Books, 1989.

John Thorn and Pete Palmer, eds. *Total Baseball*. Warner Books, 1989.

Index